A JEWISH READER

A JEWISH READER

IN TIME AND ETERNITY

———

EDITED BY NAHUM N. GLATZER

SCHOCKEN BOOKS · NEW YORK

The greater part of this book
was rendered into English by Olga Marx

SECOND, REVISED, EDITION

ACKNOWLEDGMENTS

Thanks are due to the following authors and publishers for permission to use selections from their works: The Johns Hopkins Press, for *The true Physician* from *The Jews and Medicine,* by Harry Friedenwald; the Soncino Press, for selections from *The Zohar,* tr. by H. Sperling and M. Simon; the Jewish Publication Society of America, for selections from *Hebrew Ethical Wills,* ed. by Israel Abrahams, and for the use of *The Holy Scriptures* in quoting the Bible; the Jewish Book Club, for selections from *Maimonides Said.*

Library of Congress Catalog Card No. 61-14920

Manufactured in the United States of America

PREFACE TO THE SECOND EDITION

The gratifying response to the *Jewish Reader* throughout the years has prompted the publisher to issue this new edition which, it is hoped, will make the volume available to even wider circles.

While the body of the text remains the same, an attempt has been made to correct printing errors and, at several points, to improve the English rendition. Scriptural references, that appeared as marginal notes in the original edition, have been moved to a separate appendix. A newly prepared index lists the major subjects and motifs, as well as the types of literature, represented in the book, while a list of *Suggestions for Further Reading* has also been added. Together with the biographical and bibliographical notes, they enhance the usefulness of the volume in classes, seminars, and study groups.

Yet all such aids must be considered of secondary importance. Of primary moment are the texts themselves, testimonies of a dedicated effort on the part of men in different lands and different ages to understand their heritage, their place in the world, and their aspirations. In these respects the texts speak for themselves.

N.N.G.

August 1961

CONTENTS

8　　　　　　　　　　C o n t e n t s

4

OUT OF THE DEPTHS

5

TURNING TO GOD

6

PARENTS AND CHILDREN

7

BUT BY MY SPIRIT

8

MERCY AND TRUTH

9

THE DESTINY OF ISRAEL

10

SUFFERING AND MARTYRDOM

Contents 11

PREFACE

These documents, chosen from the literature of post-biblical Judaism, offer significant examples of the way in which the Jews have looked on time and eternity. The formal efforts of the theologian alternate with the naive expressions of faith of the simple devout. Faith now speaks directly through free inspiration, and now ceremoniously through the established institutions of religion. A concern for the exigencies of practical law does not exclude flights of mystic contemplation. Israel, conceived of as a nation, does not exclude Israel, conceived of as the world. Both the needs of the individual and the will to transcend the individual find expression here; the love of this life and the longing for other-worldly perfection; the humble acceptance of fate and the accusatory outcry of a suffering community.

In general, the selections end with the pietist movement of Hasidism. Hasidic literature, created before Jewry felt the impact of modern Europe, provides a natural conclusion to the classical expression of Israel's heritage. But it must be remembered that the ideas offered here have not lost their relevance with the passing of their time. In reading some of the selections in this book, especially those that tell of Israel's endurance and Israel's will to live and serve, the reader will be conscious of contemporary events and will perceive that great concerns of the past live on.

Such a volume as this, in which so many different and complexly interrelated impulses and views are represented, can offer no mere summary of information or easy road to understanding. The reader will not find here a simple or one-sided account of the teachings of Israel. What it is hoped he may find is an insight into the wide range of thought that has gone into that tradition and the variety of the ways that were travelled towards the one goal—the

establishment of a relationship between the finite and the
infinite, between time and eternity.

These documents present a concept of human life as one
great dialogue between man and God. The reader will
sense the deep concern and reverence with which the
authors approached matters of life and spirit. He will feel
the earnestness that pervaded their quest for meaning and
significance in human life, and he will come to understand
the challenging concept of Israel as a community of men
charged with the special function of being aware of the
divine presence in the world—a community dedicated to
the task of "ordering the world under the kingdom of
God," in Zion, in the world, and through the vicissitudes
of history. He will understand, it is hoped, the deep impli-
cations of Jewish reverence for learning—learning for its
own sake, learning as a way to sanctify the divine name,
learning as a preparation for active life. Finally, he will
see in the Jewish tradition a recurrent attempt to recognize
all new ideas as originating in the Scriptures, thus making
thought and life one all-embracing commentary on the living word of God.

This book is not designed to support any doctrine. The
variety and involutions of the tradition are emphasized;
no "line" has been taken. The reader may be attracted to
certain conceptions and opposed to others. But, whether
in agreement or contradiction,—what matters is that the
reader of today should enter into a living relationship
with the men who speak in these documents. In this way
their utterances may become contemporary in the widest
sense of the word, in that they address themselves with
equal force and intent to every generation.

When not otherwise indicated in the index to the
sources, the translations are the work of Olga Marx, who
was assisted by the editor. A number of passages in the
book appear in condensed form. Translations taken over
from other publications have in some instances been
adapted to the usage of the main body of the book.

N. N. GLATZER

A JEWISH READER

BETWEEN GOD AND MAN

HOW WE SHALL SERVE

Israel Baal Shem

Podolia, 18th Century

Unless we believe that God renews the work of creation every day, our prayers and obeying of the commandments grow old and accustomed, and tedious. As it is written in the psalm: "Cast me not off in the time of old age"—that is to say, do not let my world grow old.

And in Lamentations it is written: "They are new every morning: great is Thy faithfulness." That the world is new to us every morning—that is Your great faithfulness!

GOD, WORLD, MAN

Nahman of Bratzlav

Ukraine, 18th–19th Century

THE WORLD

The world is a spinning die, and everything turns and changes: man is turned to an angel, and an angel to man; and the head to the foot, and the foot to the head. Thus all things turn and spin and change, this into that, and that into this, the topmost to the undermost, and the undermost to the topmost. For at the root all is one, and salvation inheres in the change and return of things.

SEEING THE WORLD

Just as the hand, held before the eye, can hide the tallest mountain, so this small earthly life keeps our gaze from the vast radiance and the secrets that fill the world. And he who can draw it from his eyes, as one draws away the hand, will see the great light at the core of the world.

GOD AND MAN

All distress that man experiences comes out of himself, for the light of God is always flooded about him, but man —by stressing the life of the body too much—fashions a shadow, so that the light of God cannot reach him.

FAITH

Faith is a very strong thing, and through faith and simplicity, without sophistry, a man will be found worthy to attain the state of grace, which is an even higher rung than holy wisdom. He will receive the very great and lavish grace of God in ecstatic silence, until he can endure the power of silence no longer, and cries out from the fullness of his soul.

TRUTH AND DIALECTIC

Victory cannot tolerate truth, and if that which is true is spread before your very eyes, you will reject it, because you are a victor. Whoever would have truth itself, must drive hence the spirit of victory; only then may he prepare to behold the truth.

THE WHEREFORE OF THE WORLD

The world was created only for the sake of choice and of the chooser.

Man, the master of choice, shall say: "Only for my sake was the whole world created!" Therefore every man shall be watchful, and strive to redeem the world and supply that wherein it is lacking, at all times and in all places.

HAPPINESS

Happiness settles the spirit, but melancholy sends it forth into exile.

CHOICE

No limits are set to the ascent of man, and the loftiest precincts are open to all. In this, your choice alone is supreme.

BETWEEN GOD AND MAN

from the Talmud and the Midrash

THE BLESSING

When Rabbi Johanan ben Zakkai fell ill, his disciples went to his house to visit him. They spoke to him, saying: "Master, give us your blessing."

He said to them: "May it be His will that the fear of heaven be upon you in the same measure as the fear of those who are of flesh and blood."

They asked: "Only so much?"

He answered them: "Would that it were so much! For you must know that when a man intends to commit a transgression, he says: 'If only no man sees me!' "

BIG AND SMALL

A Samaritan asked Rabbi Meir: "Is it possible that He of whom it is written 'Do not I fill heaven and earth?' spoke to Moses 'from between the two staves of the ark?' "[1]

The rabbi said to him: "Fetch me a mirror that magnifies."

He fetched such a mirror. Then the rabbi said: "Now look at yourself."

He looked at himself and saw himself magnified.

[1] The ark of the covenant, carried by means of staves, stood in the holy of holies (Exod. 25:10 ff.).

The rabbi continued: "Now fetch me a mirror that makes smaller." Then he said: "Look at yourself."

He saw himself smaller. Then the rabbi said to him: "If you, who are made of flesh and blood, can appear changed in any way you please, how much more He, who had only to speak and the world was created! Thus, if it is his will, the words hold: 'Do not I fill heaven and earth?' But if he wills otherwise, he speaks to Moses from between the two staves of the ark."

IN COMMON USE

This is a parable of a king who had a friend. The king sent word to him: "Know, that I would have a meal with you; go and prepare it for me."

His friend went about the work, preparing a couch, a candlestick, and a table such as he commonly used.

When the king arrived, his servants came with him, and from this side and that preceded him, bearing candlesticks of gold before his countenance. When his friend beheld all this splendor, he was ashamed and hid all he had prepared because it was what he commonly used.

Then the king said to him: "Did I not send word that I would have a meal with you? Why have you not prepared anything for me?"

Whereupon his friend replied: "I beheld the splendor that arrived with you, and I was ashamed and hid everything I had prepared for you because it was what I commonly use."

The king said to him: "By your life! I shall discard all I have brought, and shall use only what is yours, for the sake of our friendship."

And so: The Holy One, blessed be he, is all light, as it is written: "And the light dwelleth with Him," yet he says to Israel: "Prepare for me candlesticks and lamps," as it is written: "When thou lightest the lamps. . . ."

THE SERVICE OF GOD

"Honor the Lord with thy substance," with that which he has bestowed upon you. If you are beautiful, honor him who has made you so, fear him and praise him with the beauty he has bestowed upon you. If your voice is beautiful and you are seated in the house of prayer, rise up and honor the Lord with your voice.

Hiyya, the son of Rabbi Eliezer ha-Kappar's sister, had a beautiful voice, and his uncle was wont to say to him: "Hiyya, my son, rise up and honor the Lord with that which he has bestowed upon you."

THE RIGHTEOUS

"The Lord loveth the righteous."

Says the Holy One, blessed be he: "They love me, and I love them also." And why does the Holy One, blessed be he, love the righteous? Because their righteousness is not a matter of heritage or family.

You will find that the priests form a father's house and the Levites form a father's house, for it is said: "O house of Aaron, bless ye the Lord; O house of Levi, bless ye the Lord." A man may wish to become a priest and yet he cannot; he may wish to become a Levite and yet he cannot. And why? Because his father was no priest, or no Levite. But if a man, even a gentile, wishes to be righteous, he can be this, because the righteous do not form a house. Therefore it is said: "Ye that fear the Lord, bless ye the Lord." It is not said, house of those that fear the Lord, but ye that fear the Lord, for they form no father's house. Of their own free will, they have come forward and loved the Holy One, blessed be he. And that is why he loves them. This is what is meant by the words: "The Lord loveth the righteous."

THE DIRECTION

"And it came to pass, when Moses held up his hand, that Israel prevailed: and when he let down his hand, Amalek prevailed."

Is it then the hands of Moses that make the battle or break the battle? No, what this means is that always when Israel looked up and surrendered its heart to the Father in heaven, it prevailed, and when it did not, it fell.

And likewise it is written: "And the Lord said unto Moses, Make thee a fiery serpent, and set it upon a pole . . . and it came to pass that if a serpent had bitten any man, when he looked unto the serpent of brass, he lived." Is it then the serpent that kills or restores? No! Always when Israel looked upward and surrendered its heart to the Father in heaven, it was healed, but if it did otherwise, it was destroyed.

WAGES

Antigonus, a man of Soko, used to say: Do not be like servants who wait upon the master with an eye to receiving a gratuity, but be like servants who wait upon their master with no eye to receiving a gratuity, and let the fear of heaven be upon you.

HIS

Rabbi Eleazar of Bertota says:
Give unto God what is his—
for you and what is yours are his.
This is also expressed by David:
"For all things come of Thee,
and of Thine own have we given Thee."

THE STEPS OF MAN

"And the Lord said unto Moses . . .
Behold, I will stand before thee there upon the rock in Horeb."
The Holy One, blessed be he, said to him:
"In every place you find a mark left by the steps of men, there I am before you."

EVERY DAY

Said David the king:
I shall testify to the love of the Holy One, blessed be he, and to the benefits he confers upon Israel, hour by hour, and day by day.

Day by day, man is sold, and every day he is redeemed;
every day the soul of man is taken from him, and delivered
    to the keeper; on the morrow it is returned to him;
as it is written:
"Into Thy hand I commit my spirit:
Thou hast redeemed me, O Lord, Thou God of truth."
Every day miracles befall him, like those who went forth
    from Egypt,
every day he experiences redemption, like those who went
    forth from Egypt,
every day he is fed at the breasts of his mother,
every day he is punished for his deeds, like a child by his
    master.

THE WHOLE

Our masters said:
Even those creatures you hold superfluous in the world,
    such as flies and fleas and gnats, even they are part of the
    creation of the world.
Through all does the Holy One, blessed be he, make mani-
    fest his mission, even through the serpent, even through
    the gnat, even through the frog.

MAN AND THING

Ben Azzai used to say:
Hold no man insignificant, and no thing improbable,
for there is no man who has not his hour,
and there is no thing that has not its place.

THE FACE OF MAN

from the Zohar

Spain, 13th Century

"And the fear of you and the dread of you shall be upon every beast of the earth, and upon every fowl of the air, upon all wherewith the ground teemeth, and upon all the fishes of the sea; into your hand are they delivered": from now on [after the Flood] and in all time to come, your form shall be that of man. But in the beginning they had not the form of man.

Come, and see! From the very outset it is written: "In the image of God made He man." And it is written: "In the day that God created man, in the likeness of God made He him." But after they had sinned, their form was changed, away from that supernal form, and was so altered that they were afraid of the wild creatures of earth.

In the beginning, all the creatures in the world lifted their eyes and beheld the holy form above, and trembled and feared it. But when they had sinned their form was changed into another form, changed so that men tremble and fear the other creatures of earth.

Come, and see! When man does not sin before his Lord, does not transgress the precepts of the Torah, the radiance of his form does not change and grow different from the image of that supernal form, and all the creatures in the world tremble and fear him. But at the hour that men transgress the words of the Torah, their form is changed and they all tremble and fear the other creatures, just because the heavenly form was changed and taken from them. And so the wild creature on earth has power over them, because it does not behold the supernal form, as it once beheld it.

But now [after the Flood] that the world became new, as in the beginning, He blessed them with His blessing and gave them power over everything, as it says: "And. . . all the fishes of the sea: into your hand are they delivered"— even the fishes of the sea!

DESIGN IN THE UNIVERSE

Moses Maimonides

Spain—Egypt, 12th Century

FROM MOREH NEBUKIM

Very often the throngs of the unreasonable will, in their hearts, put forth the claim that there is more evil than good in this world, so that in a great number of proverbs and poems of most peoples, it appears as though finding good anywhere were almost a miracle, and as though evil prevailed and endured. This error is not confined to the unreasonable, but is common even among those who consider themselves wise. Thus Al-Razi,[1] in his famous book, which he called *On Metaphysics*, collected many of his absurd and foolish ideas, and among them a concept he made up for himself, namely, that more evil exists than good. For if you compare the well-being of man and his joys in times of ease with the sum of his pain, bitter grief, debility, the destruction of his organs, his unrest, cares, fears, you will find that the existence of man is beset by distress and much evil. And then he sets out to prove the truth of this opinion by enumerating evils, one after another, in juxtaposition to that which truth-loving men think concerning the grace of God and his manifest mercy, and concerning the fact that he, exalted be his name, is beyond doubt perfect goodness, and that everything which comes from him is perfect goodness.

But the cause of this error is that this foolish man and his unreasonable companions in the throng regard the whole universe only from the angle of individual existence. Thus every fool thinks that life is there for his sake alone, and as though nothing existed but he. And so, when anything happens that opposes his wishes, he concludes that the whole universe is evil. But if man would regard the whole universe itself and realize what an infinitesimal part he plays in it, the truth would be clear and apparent to him. He would see that men have formulated the stupid

[1] Arabian physician and philosopher of the 10th century.

generality of the prevalence of evil in this world (which they have thought up for themselves) not with regard to the Divine Messengers,[1] or to the spheres and stars, or to the elements and whatever is composed of them, or to stones and plants, or to the species of other living things, but with regard to some particular instance in mankind.

But the truth of the matter is that all living men, and even more all other species of living creatures, are out of all proportion to the permanent universe. As it is clearly said in the Scriptures: "Man is like unto a breath"; "The nations are as a drop of a bucket, and are counted as the small dust of the balance." It is of great advantage that man recognize the measure of his worth, so that he may not fall into the error of believing that the universe exists only because of him. It is our opinion that the universe exists only for the sake of the Creator, and that in it the species of man is very small indeed compared to the higher portion of the universe, to the spheres and the stars. And valued in comparison with the Divine Messengers—but how can we even begin to compare these two! Yet man is the most important of all the creatures in this lower world—what I mean is, among everything made up of the elements—and so his life is a great treasure and a grace of God by which he has distinguished man.

Most of the evil that befalls individuals comes from the imperfections within themselves. Out of these imperfections of ours we cry out demands. The evil we inflict upon ourselves, of our own volition, and which pains us, this evil we ascribe to God. How very remote from him it is! As it is clearly expressed in his Book: "Is corruption His? No; His children's is the blemish; a generation crooked and perverse."

In order to demonstrate this, let us group all the evils that may befall men, in three categories.

The first category consists of the evils that befall man from the very nature of being born and dying—what I mean is, from the very fact that he is made of mortal stuff.

1 The usual translation is "angel." The Hebrew word, however, denotes any being or natural force employed by God for the execution of his message.

Thus some men have grave ailments, or their organs are destroyed either at birth or later through changes that affect the elements themselves, through impure air, through violent tempests, or through the ground yielding from under their dwellings. We have already demonstrated that divine wisdom has made it a necessity that only through death can there be life, and that without the death of the individual, the life of the species cannot continue. And so you may well see how perfect is His grace and His mercy. But he who is made of flesh and bone and yet does not wish to be subject to that to which all matter is subject, is trying to reconcile two contrasts without realizing it: he wants to be subject and not subject to change. For were he not subject to change, there could be no generation; there would be one single being, but it could not constitute the individual of a species.

But you will find that the evils of this category that befall men are very rare, and occur only at long intervals. You will find lands where the ground has not sunk in centuries and where there have been no conflagrations. Likewise, thousands of persons are born in the best of health, and the birth of an ailing child is a rare event and a special case, or—if some obstinate person should be insistent and refuse to admit that it is nothing but a special case—it is, at any rate, a seldom occurrence that does not involve even the hundredth, no, the thousandth part of all those who are born in perfection.

The second category consists of the evils that men inflict upon one another, in that they use violence against one another. This evil is more frequently encountered than the evils in the first category, and the reasons are numerous and well known; they too lie within ourselves, yet no amount of wisdom can obviate them. However, there is no country in the world among whose inhabitants this category of evil is very widely spread. It is rare, and we find it only where a man schemes against another, to murder him or to steal his money by night. It is true that in great wars this category of evils affects many people; but this too does not occur in the major part of the inhabited earth.

The third category of evil is that which may affect a man as a consequence of his own doings. And this category is the one found most frequently. The evil in it is far more frequent than that in the second category. The evil included in this category affects all men, so that they cry aloud, and this is because there is none who has not sinned against himself, be it in ever so slight a measure. For this category is made up of all the objectionable qualities of man, such as excessive greed for food and drink and the act of begetting, or too great an indulgence in these and the disturbing of their proper order, or eating of bad food. This is the cause of all sickness and of the blows that strike the body or the soul. This is easy to see in the sicknesses that affect the body. But the sicknesses of the soul derive from this evil in two respects. The first: The changes that the soul undergoes necessarily spring from the changes of the body, since the soul is a power dwelling in the body, for it has already been said that the qualities of the soul have their origin in the condition of the body.[1] The second: The soul is apt to become accustomed to that which is not necessary, and acquires the definite characteristic of striving for what is not necessary either to maintain the individual or to preserve the species. And this striving can find no goal for itself. For the amount of the necessary can be attained, and what is necessary has a goal. But whatever is superfluous can find no goal.

But the worthy and the wise recognize the wisdom embodied in the universe and understand it, as it is expressed by David: "All the paths of the Lord are mercy and truth unto such as keep His covenant and His testimonies." What he means by this is that those who have regard for the nature of the universe and for the commandments in the Torah and the goal of these commandments, clearly behold mercy and truth, and so they set up as their goal that which is intended for them as human beings—understanding. And to satisfy the needs of the body, they seek only the necessary things, "bread to eat and raiment to put on," and nothing that is superfluous. Now this is quite simple and everyone could attain to it with small effort— were he content with what is necessary! But what seems difficult to you in this connection, too difficult and too

1 Moreh Nebukim II. 36.

burdensome for us, is only because of the superfluous. For if you seek after what is not necessary, it will become difficult to find even what is necessary, and the more men desire what is superfluous, the more difficult this thing becomes. Not only are strength and possessions corroded by what is unnecessary, but even what is necessary is lacking!

It is important for you to observe how nature proves the validity of our words. The more important a thing is for living creatures, the more common and the cheaper it is, and all that is less necessary, and hence less important, is rarer and more costly. To give an example: The most necessary things for man are air, water, and food. And of these, air is of the greatest importance, for if he had to do without it for even the fraction of an hour, he would die. And water—he might be able to live without it for a day or two. Thus air is present in the greatest quantity and is cheapest. Water is more important than food, for there are people who could exist without food for four or five days, provided they were given drink. And in every land, water is more common and cheaper than food. And all this applies to food itself: the most important foods everywhere are most abundant and cheaper than those which are less necessary. Musk and ambergris, rubies and emeralds—I do not think that anyone with perfect understanding could believe these are necessary to man, unless it be as a means of therapy, although divers herbs and various stones could be used in their stead, or in the stead of things like them.

This is a revelation of the mercy of God, blessed be he, a mercy conferred on all life down to the frailest of living creatures. And his righteousness and justice regarding animals are manifest, for in the entire natural cycle of living and dying there is no single creature among all kinds of animals that becomes something extraordinary through an extraordinary endowment, or because an extra limb is added. No, all physical and psychic powers, all vital forces and all limbs bestowed on one creature, are likewise bestowed on the other. And if any lacks something, this is a lack that has come about afterward, and is not according to nature, and it is a seldom occurrence, as we have demonstrated.

In the light of these two considerations, you will clearly see the mercy of God to his creatures, blessed be he; for he gave being to the necessary in accordance with its laws, and he created all the individuals of a certain species alike. And with this truth in mind, the master among the prophets said: "For all His ways are justice . . . just and right is He." And David said: "All the paths of the Lord are mercy and truth," and David expresses it still more definitely in the words: "The Lord is good to all and His tender mercies are over all His works." For that he has given us life, that is the great and perfect good, as we have demonstrated; and the creation of the power which guides the animals, that is the mercy which is shown them, as we have demonstrated.

DOOR WITHIN DOOR

from the Zohar

Spain, 13th Century

"And Sarah heard in the tent door, which was behind him."

Rabbi Judah began a discourse with the verse: "Her husband is known in the gates, when he sitteth among the elders of the land." He said:

The Holy One, blessed be he, is transcendent in his glory, he is hidden and removed far beyond all ken; there is no one in the world, nor has there ever been one whom his wisdom and essence do not elude, since he is recondite and hidden and beyond all ken, so that neither the supernal nor the lower beings are able to commune with him until they utter the words: "Blessed be the glory of the Lord from His place."

The creatures of the earth think of him as being on high, declaring, "His glory is above the heavens," while the heavenly beings think of him as being below, declaring,

"His glory is over all the earth," until they both, in heaven and on earth, concur in declaring: "Blessed be the glory of the Lord from His place," because he is unknowable and no one can truly understand him.

This being so, how can you say: "Her husband is known in the gates"? But of a truth the Holy One makes himself known to every one according to the measure of his understanding and his capacity to attach himself to the spirit of divine wisdom; a full knowledge is beyond the reach of any being.

Rabbi Simeon said:

The "gates" mentioned in this passage are the same as the gates in the passage, "Lift up your heads, O ye gates," and refer to the supernal grades by and through which alone a knowledge of the Almighty is possible to man, and but for which man could not commune with God. Similarly, man's soul cannot be known directly, save through the members of the body, which are the grades forming the instruments of the soul. The soul is thus known and unknown. So it is with the Holy One, blessed be he, since he is the Soul of souls, the Spirit of spirits, covered and veiled from every one; nevertheless, through these gates, which are doors for the soul, the Holy One makes himself known.

For there is door within door, grade behind grade, through which the glory of the Holy One is made known. Hence here the "tent door" is the door of righteousness, referred to in the words, "Open to me the gates of righteousness," and this is the first entrance door: through this door a view is opened to all the other supernal doors. He who succeeds in entering this door is privileged to know both it and all the other doors, since they all repose on this one.

At the present time this door remains unknown because Israel is in exile; and therefore all the other doors are removed from them, so that they cannot know or commune; but when Israel will return from exile, all the supernal grades are destined to rest harmoniously upon this one. Then men will obtain a knowledge of the precious supernal wisdom of which hitherto they knew not, as it is written: "And the spirit of the Lord shall rest upon him, the spirit of wisdom and understanding, the spirit of counsel and might, the spirit of knowledge and of the fear of the Lord."

PEACE

Perek ha-Shalom

Palestine, 1st–3rd Century

Rabbi Joshua ben Levi said: Great is peace, because peace is to the earth what yeast is to the dough. If the Holy One, blessed be he, had not given peace to the earth, it would be depopulated by the sword and by hosts of animals.

In Palestine we learn: Rabban Simeon ben Gamaliel said: The world rests upon three things: On justice, on truth, on peace. Said Rabbi Mona: Those three are one and the same thing. For if there is justice, there is truth, and there is peace. And these three are expressed in one and the same verse of the Scriptures, for it is written: "Execute the judgment of truth and peace in your gates." Wherever there is justice, there is peace, and wherever there is peace, there is justice.

Rabbi Jose the Galilean says: The name of the Anointed too is peace; as it is written: "God the mighty, the Everlasting Father, the Ruler of peace."

Rabbi Jose the Galilean says: Great is peace—for at the hour the Anointed King reveals himself unto Israel, he will begin in no other way than with "peace." As it is written: "How beautiful upon the mountains are the feet of the messenger of good tidings, that announceth peace."

Rabbi Jose the Galilean says: Great is peace, for even in the hour of war, we begin in no other way than with "peace." For it is written: "When thou drawest nigh unto a city to fight against it, then proclaim peace unto it."

Rabban Simeon ben Gamaliel says: Great is peace, for
Aaron the priest was praised only because he was a
peaceable man. For it was he who loved peace, who pursued peace, who was first to offer peace, and who responded
to peace; as it is written: "He walked with Me in peace
and uprightness." And what is written thereafter? "And
did turn many away from iniquity." This teaches: If ever
he saw two men who hated each other, he went to one of
them and said to him: "Why do you hate that man? For
he came to my house, and prostrated himself before me
and said: 'I have sinned against him!' Go and pacify
him!" And Aaron left him and went to the second man
and spoke to him as to the first. Thus it was his wont to
set peace and love and friendship between man and man,
and he 'did turn many away from iniquity.'

Rabbi Joshua of Siknin spoke in the name of Rabbi
Levi: Great is peace, for we seal all benedictions and all
prayers with "peace." The recitation of the Shema [1] we seal
with "peace": "Spread the tabernacle of peace." [2] The
benediction of the priest is sealed with "peace": "And give
thee peace." All benedictions are sealed with "peace": "He
who makes peace."

Said Rabbi Joshua ben Levi: Thus spake the Holy One,
blessed be he, to Israel: "You have caused my house to be
destroyed and my children to be banished—but ask for
Jerusalem's peace and I shall forgive you." He, however,
who loves peace, who pursues peace, who offers peace first,
and responds to peace, the Holy One, blessed be he, will
let him inherit the life of this world and the coming world,
as it is written: "But the humble shall inherit the land,
and delight themselves in the abundance of peace."

[1] "Hear, O Israel," core of the morning and evening prayers, consisting
of the following passages: Deut. 6:4–9, 11:13–21; Num. 15:37–41.
[2] Evening prayer.

THE PURE IN HEART

ON HIDING FROM THE PRESENCE
OF GOD

Philo

Egypt, 1st Century

FROM LEGUM SACRARUM ALLEGORIARUM LIBRI

"And Adam and his wife hid themselves from the presence
of the Lord God amongst the trees of the garden." Here
the Scriptures acquaint us with the principle that the
wicked are homeless.[1] For if virtue constitutes the true
city of the wise, then he who cannot participate in virtue
is an exile from that city. And the wicked cannot participate in virtue, and so they are exiled, they are fugitives.
But he who flees from virtue, at once hides himself from
God. For if the wise are visible to God—since they are his
friends—the wicked are apparently all hidden and con-
cealed from him, since they are evil enemies of right
reason. The Scriptures testify that the wicked man has no
home and no habitation, in the allusion to Esau in his
"hairy mantle" and guise of sinfulness, for it is said: "Esau
was a cunning hunter, a man of the field." For wickedness

---

1 The double meanings of *polis* ("city," and "state"), and of *pheugein*
("to flee," "to be exiled," hence "to be outlawed") clarify this passage.
To understand what follows, it must be borne in mind that according
to the teachings of the Cynics and the Stoics, the wise man does not
regard himself as a citizen of any single state, but as a member of
the world state. Citizenship in this world state, however, is based on
the possession of the quality of reason; Philo interprets this ethically.

bound on the hunt for passions, and foolishly hastening in pursuit of boorishness,[1] cannot live in the city of virtue. Jacob, on the other hand, who is full of wisdom, is a citizen of virtue and dwells in virtue, for of him it is said: "And Jacob was a quiet man, dwelling in tents." And this is also the reason why it is said: "And it came to pass, because the midwives feared God, that they made themselves *houses*." [2] For such [souls] as seek out the hidden secrets of God—and that means "bringing the male children to the birth"—build up the works of virtue in which they choose to dwell. And so it is shown herewith in what sense the wicked are without a home and without a habitation, since they are exiled from the precincts of virtue, while the good have received wisdom as their house and as their city.

Now we shall investigate in what sense it can be said of a person that he is hiding from God. It is impossible to understand these words we have before us in the Scriptures, unless we give them an allegorical interpretation. For God fills and penetrates everything; he has left nothing empty and void of his presence. How then could anyone be in a place where God is not? Another passage of the Scriptures testifies to this: "The Lord, He is God in heaven above, and upon the earth beneath; there is none else." And further on: "Behold, I will stand before thee." For before anything was created, there was God, and he is found everywhere, so that no one can hide from him. Why should this fill us with wonder? We could not escape from the elements of all things created, even if we had cause to wish to hide from them. Just try to flee from water and air, from the sky or from the whole of the world! We are, of necessity, caught in their compass, for no one can flee from the world. But if we cannot hide from parts of the world, and from the world itself, how then could we hide from the presence of God? Never! So what is meant by the

---

1 This is an allusion to the third meaning of *polis*—the urban in contrast to the rural. The Greeks considered the peasant (*agroikos*) uneducated, just as the Jews so regarded the Am ha-Arez, and the Romans the *rusticus*.
2 Exod. 1:21. This is the reading of the Septuagint. The Hebrew text reads: "He [God] made them houses."

expression "hid themselves"? The wicked believe that God is in a certain place, that he does not encompass, but that he is encompassed. And so they think they can hide, because the Creator of all life is not in that part of the world which they have selected for their hiding place.

Thus we have shown in what way the wicked are fugitives and hide from God. Now we shall see where they hide. "Amongst the trees of the garden" is what we read, that is, in the center of the mind, which is, so to speak, in the middle of the garden, that is, of the whole soul. He who flees from God, flees into himself. For there are two kinds of mind, the mind of the universe, and that is God, and the mind of individual man. And the one flees from his own mind to the mind of the universe—for whoever leaves his own mind, avows therewith that the works of the mortal mind are as nothing, and ascribes everything to God. But the other flees from God, and declares that not God is the cause of anything at all, but that he himself is the cause of all that comes to pass. Thus there are many who believe that all the things in the world go their own course by themselves, without a guide, and that it is the spirit of man that has invented the arts, crafts, laws, customs, state institutions, and the rights of the individual and the community, both in regard to men and to beasts, that are without reason.[1] But you, O my soul, see the difference between these two points of view. For the one leaves the perishable mortal mind, which has been created, and chooses for its true aid the primordial and immortal mind of the universe. But the other, which sets aside God, foolishly courts as its ally the human mind, which is not even able to help itself.

[1] This gives an approximate picture of the Epicurean point of view.

THE GOOD NAME

Sayings of the Talmudic Masters

THE END OF MAN

Thus spoke Rabbi Meir, when he had ended the Book
   of Job:
The end of man is death,
the end of cattle is slaughter.
Everything that is, dies.
Happy is he who has grown in the Torah,
whose labors are concerned with the Torah,
who gives satisfaction to his Maker,
who has grown up with a good name,
and with a good name departs from this world.
About him Solomon says:
"A good name
is better than precious oil;
and the day of death
than the day of one's birth."

I WILL BE WITH YOU

Rabbi Meir was wont to say:
Learn with all your heart, and with all your soul,
to know My ways,
to watch at the gates of My Torah.
Keep My Torah in your heart,
before your eyes keep the fear of Me;
guard your mouth from all sin,
purify yourself from faults and transgressions,
and make yourself holy,
and I will be with you in every place.

FELLOW MAN

The Masters of Jabneh were wont to say:
I am a creature, and my fellow man is a creature.
As for me—my work is in the city.

As for him—his work is in the field.
I rise early to go to my work,
and he rises early to go to his work.
As he does not feel superior to my work,
so do I not feel superior to his work.
And should you perhaps say,
that I do more, and he does less—
We have learned:
"The one more, the other less—if only his heart is turned
    to heaven." [1]

BROTHERS

Abbaye was wont to say:
Let man ever be inventive in the fear of God,
giving a soft answer that turneth away wrath.
Let him increase the peace with his brothers, with his
    relatives, and with every man,
even with the stranger in the market place,
that he may be beloved above and desired below,
and well received by all creatures.

THE FINAL GOAL

Raba was wont to say:
The final goal of wisdom is to turn to God and to do good
    works.
So that a man may not read the Torah and learn the
    Tradition
and then set foot on his father, or his mother,
or his master, or on him who is greater than he in wisdom
    and in years.
Thus it is said:
"The fear of the Lord is the beginning of wisdom;
a good understanding have all they that do thereafter."

[1] Menahot 110 a.

THE DEVOUT

Judah ha-Levi

Spain—Palestine, 11th–12th Century

FROM THE KUZARI

The Chazar king said: Tell me what a devout man among you does in this present era.

The master said: The devout man bends his thought upon his state. For all of its inhabitants he weighs out and distributes food and that which they need. He deals with them justly; never would he oppress anyone, but neither would he give him more than the portion accruing to him. That is why he finds them obedient to his wishes the moment he needs them, and eager to respond the moment he calls. He gives them commands and they do according to his commands; he gives them prohibitions and they abide by his prohibitions.

The Chazar king said: I asked you to tell me about a devout man, not about a ruler.

The master replied: The devout man *is* a ruler, who is obeyed by his senses and his powers, both the spiritual and the physical. The devout man would indeed have the right to rule, for if he ruled a country, his rule would be equally just as that which he practices over his body and soul.

For he shackles the passions and dams them in, after he has given them their portion and that which they need in the way of sufficient food and drink—always keeping the golden mean, and in the way of cleanness, and everything needful for this, also keeping the golden mean. He also shackles the forces that crave power and strive toward superiority after he has given them their portion in the way of beneficent superiority in matters of wisdom, of knowledge, and the warding off of evil persons. He gives to each of the senses that portion which is good for it. He uses his hands, his feet, and his tongue only for what is necessary, and for a good purpose. It is the same with his hearing and his sight, and the related feelings that attend them; with imagination and the power of judgment, the power to think, and memory; and with the power of will, which employs all of these others. All of these are nothing but servants, subject to the will of reason. But he does not permit one or the other of these forces and limbs to exceed in that for which it is destined, and thus to thrust back the rest.

When he has satisfied the needs of each of these, when he has given the vegetative forces enough rest and sleep, and the animal forces enough of waking and movement through worldly activities, then he calls up his people like a ruler who summons an obedient host, so that his people may help him reach a higher step, the divine step that is higher than the step of reason. He arranges his community in a certain order, as Moses, peace be with him, ranged his people around Mount Sinai. He bids will power receive every command that comes from him, to obey, to carry it out immediately and without rebelliousness, and to employ powers and limbs in accordance with his command. He bids it turn away from the tempters of mind and imagination, not to take on anything from them, and not to believe anything without consulting with reason. And if reason thinks that what these others want is right, let it be accepted; if not, let it be rejected.

The will accepts these biddings and agrees to fulfill them. He instructs all the organs of thinking in this matter; and here he clears away all worldly thoughts mentioned above. Imagination is ordered to put at his disposal, with the aid of memory, whatever splendid images it beholds, in order to resemble the divine toward which he is striving—what came to pass on Mount Sinai, for instance, or the binding of Isaac on Mount Moriah, the Tabernacle that Moses erected, the Temple, the descent of the glory of God on the house of holiness, and much else. And he bids memory, which preserves, to preserve all this, and not to forget it. He forbids the mind and its tempters to confuse truth and to make it doubtful. He forbids overbearingness and greed to influence or to disturb will power or to goad it on through force and desire.

The words of the tongue coincide with the thought, without adding anything to it. It does not recite prayers out of mere custom and habit, like a starling or a parrot, but with meaning and piety in every word. This hour becomes the heart and fruit of his lifetime, and all other hours are only as paths that lead to it. He longs for this hour to arrive, for in it he comes to resemble what is spiritual and grows remote from what is animal. And so the hours of the three prayers are the fruit of his day and night, but the fruit of the week is the Sabbath, because it is appointed for coming close to the divine and its service, not in humiliation but in joy.

THE WORLD OF THOSE WHO LOVE GOD

Bahya ibn Pakuda

Spain, 11th–12th Century

FROM HOBOT HA-LEBABOT

The habits of those who love God are too many to be enumerated, and so I shall speak of those which occur to me.

These are the men who have knowledge of their God, who perceive that he delights in them and leads them, that he guides them and sustains them, that everything he gave them permission to occupy themselves with, whether it be concerned with the Torah or with the world, is under his government and will. And so it becomes clear to them, and they trust in it, that all their concerns and impulses are guided according to the decision of the Creator, exalted be he, and according to his desire. Thus they desist from choosing one thing and preferring it to another, and are certain that their Creator will choose for them what is good and right.

And since from the Torah it becomes apparent to them that through the commandments God has made them look to their actions and ordered them to choose the service of the Creator, but that he has barred them from choosing indulgence—since all this becomes apparent to

them—they choose to be in that place where he has put
them, to thirst for him, to yearn for his approval with their
hearts and their most secret selves, and to desist from
yearning for the world and its turmoil. With all their
hearts, with all their souls, they look to him for help and
strength to make real their thoughts in his service, and to
perfect the deed they have chosen from those included in
his commandments. But if they achieve some deed, they
praise God for this, and they give him thanks, while he
praises them because of their effort and their choice. But
when, through their powerlessness to reach him, they do
not succeed in bodying forth their thoughts, they apologize
to God for this, and determine to do it at a time when
they are able. And so they await this time, which the
Creator will with his help accord them, and implore him
for it with pure soul and faithful heart. This is the goal
of their desires, the end of their wishes to God, as David,
peace be with him, has said: "Oh that my ways were directed to observe Thy statutes!" And the Creator praises
them for choosing to serve him, even if it is denied them
to make the deed materialize, for he said to David:
"Whereas it was in thy heart to build an house for My
name, thou didst well that it was in thy heart."

And so in their hearts and in their thoughts, they aban-
don the things of this world, and the concern for the body,
and only at such times as it is necessary to satisfy its needs
are their bodily senses concerned with it, because they
regard this as contemptible, it is trivial in their eyes. And
so they turn their hearts and their souls to the matters in
the Torah and to the serving of God, to glorifying and
exalting him, and to doing his commandments. Thus their
bodies are of this world but their hearts are of the spirit.
And so they serve God with that which their hearts have
of awareness of him, and participate, as it were, in the
service of the Holy Messengers in the heaven above the
heavens. Desires melt from their hearts, the ground is
taken away from under the yearning for indulgence, because they have learned something of the yearning to
serve the Creator, something of the love for him. The
fires of [evil] urge are extinguished in their hearts, its
glow is put out in their thoughts, before the powerful

light of service that suffuses them, just as comes to pass
with a lamp in the light of the sun. They are bowed down
in the fear of God. Before him, they confess how small
they are, and they bow down in his service, unconcerned
for what they lack.

When you deal with them, they seem to you the brothers
of modesty; when you talk with them, they appear to you
as sages; when you question them, as scholars; when you
sin against them, as the meek. You see their forms: they
are bathed in light. And if you search their hearts, you will
find a heart broken before God. In communing with him,
they are at home; in the business of the world, they are
silent. Their hearts are filled with the love of God, but
not with desire for the doing of men, and not with pleasure
in their talk. They spurn the road of corruption and go
on the most elect of all paths. It is their merit that suffering
departs, that rain falls; and that men and beasts have water
is their merit, because they have denied their bodies forbidden union, they have kept their hands from all manner
of indulgences, and their souls have fled from what is forbidden in order to go the good and straight path. And so
by suffering only few days, they attain to high rank, and
acquire both worlds; they garner both kinds of good, and
they receive both advantages in full. As it is said in the
psalm: "Happy is the man that feareth the Lord, that
delighteth greatly in His commandments," and so to the
end. And an extraordinary thing about them is that in
their eyes the commandments that their Creator summons
them to do are too few, in comparison to the duties that
would be in measure with the good he has done for them,
or in comparison to what their souls have assumed in the
way of effort, and striving, and enduring, and patience, in
order to cling in his service. And this is as I shall tell you:

For they count the commandments of the Creator, of
which there are six hundred and thirteen; and of these
three hundred and sixty-five are prohibitory laws, and of
the mandatory laws, which only the community is obliged
to observe, not the individual, there are sixty-five. Furthermore, of the mandatory laws, there are those which are
confined only to certain times, like Sabbaths, and feasts,
and fasts. Furthermore, some of the mandatory laws are

valid only in the Holy Land—such as those regarding individual sacrifices, offerings and tithes, the pilgrimages to
Jerusalem, and the like. Furthermore, there are those
commandments which depend purely on special occasions.
If these occasions arise, it is one's duty to obey the injunc-
tions; if they do not arise, the commandments need not be
done—as, for instance, the commandment of circumcision
as concerns a man who has no son, the redemption of the
first-born as concerns one who has no first-born son, the
injunction to make a parapet for the roof as concerns him
who builds no house, the commandment to honor father
and mother as concerns an orphan, and the like. And when
they have counted the commandments in this wise, they
tell themselves: We cannot include the prohibitions, because obeying them and doing what they prescribe consists only in refraining.

And so in their eyes the service of God and their doing
seems trivial in comparison with their desire and their
longing for that which would enable them to win the approval of God. Therefore they seek out those commandments among the "duties of the limbs" that it might be
incumbent upon the individual to do at all times, in every
place, and on every occasion. But the only one of this kind
they find is the reading of the Torah and the learning of
the commandments, as it is said, "And these words, which
I command thee this day, shall be upon thy heart. And
thou shalt teach them diligently unto thy children"; and
as the prophet urges this thing a second time, "And ye
shall teach them your children, talking of them." All this
grows too trivial in their eyes, when they consider the
magnitude of that which has been revealed to them in respect to the service and the actions which they owe the
Creator, blessed be he. And so they serve the Creator by
doing commandments of reason, by extraordinary disci-
pline, and by a good spiritual conduct of life; and by these
things they add to the known commandments, because they
have pure hearts devoted to God. And so they learn the
ways of the prophets and the habits of the devout, in order
thus to seek the approval of God, and in order to be accepted by him. This, however, belongs to the "duties of the
heart," to which we have turned our attention so that in

this book we may explain their roots and consider their reaches.

For it is this accumulated wisdom that is stored in the hearts of the wise, that is cherished in their bosoms. And when they speak about it, its justice does not remain hidden, for all men of rare and extraordinary knowledge testify to its truth and its justice. But therewith they attain to a lofty grade and high rank in the service of God—that service performed out of tranquil heart, out of love for him, faithful love, proffered with heart and soul, with body and possessions, as the prophet, peace be with him, bade when he said: "And thou shalt love the Lord thy God with all thy heart, and with all thy soul, and with all thy might." And the men who have reached this stage, are among all men nearest the stage of the prophets, of the purified, the pure, the devout, whom the Scriptures call "lovers of God and lovers of His name," concerning whom it is said: "That I may cause those that love me to inherit substance; and that I may fill their treasuries."

And you, my brother, if you desire them as your companions, if you wish to join their circle, leave the superfluities of your world, keep away from these! Be content with what suffices to nourish you, and learn to live without nourishment also, and lighten the burden of worldly business that weighs your soul, and turn aside your heart, lest its thoughts plunge into the things of this world. And if you pursue those things which are necessary to you, do so with your body only, and not with your heart and your will, like one who drinks a bitter medicine: he drinks with his mouth only, not with his will, for the drinking in itself is repugnant to him, but he endures the bitterness without ado, since it serves to rid him of harm—thus should the necessities of your world appear in your eyes.

And you are already aware, my brother, that reflecting on the things of this world adds nothing to your subsistence, while it is also true that less of striving and haste will not lessen the portion decreed for you. But if you allow your heart to be distracted, it will be denied you to think your thoughts over what would benefit you in the teachings of the Torah and the commandments of the Creator, which were transmitted to you and which

you accepted, agreeing to occupy yourself with them all
the days of your life; and you would forfeit all this, de-
riving no benefits from it. But set this goal for your soul,
wherein is your salvation and the fulfillment of your Torah
and your world: use your discernment to keep far from
evil ways with all your might, and first and foremost in
your eyes be zeal for what pertains to your future. Make
discernment your king, humility your guide, wisdom your
leader, seclusion your friend. Betake yourself to the gardens of good ways, slowly and patiently, according to what
your condition makes possible. And be forewarned of ex-
cess that knows not step by step, and of distractions, so that
you may not lose yourself; for if there is too much oil in
the lamp, the light will go out. But be forewarned as well
of evasion, of indolence, and of slackness; rather, let zeal
follow upon zeal, step for step, let suffering be followed
by new suffering, add to every step of the good way that
which is above it, and do not evade examining your heart,
but think of it constantly with your soul.

And occupy yourself with reflecting on this book of
mine; read it, remember what it contains, take to heart
its maxims, and follow in the paths of its deductions, and
you will attain to the longed-for stage, the final goal of
the noble way that has the approval of God. Be upright
upon this way and try to make others upright. But your
soul cannot expect to attain this until you have turned
your heart away from the cares and distractions of this
world, nay more, until you have spurned them; for it is
not well possible for a drunken man to be healed of wine
until he has emptied it from him. One of the devout has
said: If we felt shame in the presence of our Creator, we
should not cherish the love for this world. But we are
drunk with the draught of love for this world.

And so, my brother, strive to turn your heart away from
the world, until your body also turns from its concerns.
For when the body is solitary, the spirit should also be
solitary, because thinking is knotted in with the concerns
of the world even when the body has turned from them
and has ceased occupation with them. And so, my brother,
examine your soul constantly, and labor to remove from
your heart the desire for the world; barter this desire for

future welfare, for the duties of the heart. See to it that your striving is always permeated with these duties and you will win the approval of the Creator, blessed be he; he will "make his face shine upon thee," he will accept your good deeds, and forgive your trespass, and you will find favor in his eyes, as it is said: "I love them that love me; and those that seek me earnestly shall find me."

FOR THE SAKE OF TRUTH

Moses Maimonides

Spain—Egypt, 12th Century

FROM HIS COMMENTARY ON THE MISHNAH

But you who meditate upon this book, do but understand the parable I relate, and you will make your heart intent on grasping my words about all of this. Imagine that they are bringing a little boy to the teacher, so that he teach him the Torah. This is of great benefit to the boy, because he will attain something of perfection. But because he is young in years, and his ability to comprehend is still weak, he cannot understand the degree of this benefit, nor what he will attain in the way of perfection by these means. And so his teacher, who is more mature than he, needs must goad him on to learn with things that are dear to him according to his tender age. He will say to him: "Read, and I shall give you nuts, or figs"; or "I shall give you some honey." And so he reads and makes an effort, not for the sake of the reading itself, whose worth he does not know, but so that his teacher will give him the promised things to eat. And the eating of these delicacies is more splendid in his eyes than the reading, and far more desirable to him—beyond a doubt. And therefore he must consider learning laborious and difficult. He makes an effort so that through this effort he may attain a goal that seems desirable to him, and this is a nut or a slice of honeycomb.

As he grows older and his ability to comprehend becomes stronger, and things that were important to him before grow slight in his eyes, and he desires something else, his teacher must goad him on and rouse his pleasure in learning through something that he now considers beautiful. And so his teacher will say to him: "Read, and I shall buy you fine shoes or fine garments." And so he makes an effort to read, not for the sake of learning in itself, but because of that promised clothing. And every piece of apparel is, in his eyes, more important than the Torah; it is the aim of his reading.

But when his ability to comprehend becomes more mature, and these things also seem insignificant in his eyes, and when he directs his soul to something that is still greater, then his master will say to him: "Learn this paragraph or this passage, and I shall give you a dinar or two dinars." And he reads and strives in order to receive the money; and this is more important to him than learning, because the aim of his learning is to attain the money that was promised him.

As his knowledge increases and this standard grows trivial in his eyes, and he realizes that it is a slight thing, he will desire something of more importance, and his master will say to him: "Learn, so that you may become an elder and a judge, that the people honor you and rise before you, as they do before this one and that." Thus he reads and strives in order to attain this step; and his aim is to have people show him honor, to have them praise and exalt him.

All this is contemptible. But since man's ability to comprehend is small, he must needs set up another thing than wisdom as the goal of wisdom, and be able to say to himself: "To what end are we learning? Only to attain an honor!" This, however, is veriest folly! The wise men called learning of this sort "not for its own sake,"[1] that is to say, a man does the commandments, and learns and makes an effort anent the Torah, yet not for the thing itself, but for the sake of another thing. Thus did the sages

1 Pesahim 50 b: cf. end of passage.

caution and say: "Do not make it into a diadem wherewith
to boast, and not into a hoe wherewith to dig." [1] With this
they imply what I have explained to you—that wisdom
must not be pursued with a motive, not in order to obtain
honors from men, not to gain money, and not to provide
for oneself by the study of God's Torah, blessed be he.
A man should have no purpose in the learning of wisdom
save only this—to learn to know wisdom itself. Similarly,
no purpose must be connected with truth, save that one
should know what is true. And the Torah is truth and the
purpose of knowing it is to live by it.

A perfect man should not say: If I do these commandments and hence what is good, and if I avoid transgressions
and hence what is evil, which God, blessed be he, has forbidden to do, what then is the reward I shall obtain for
this? For that would be like the boy's saying: "If I read
this, what will be given me?" And one answers him:
"This!" Since we see that his ability to comprehend is
small, and that he cannot gauge the right thing and seeks
for another goal, we answer him according to his folly;
as it is said: "Answer a fool according to his folly."

Thus even the sages cautioned that man must not set
up one thing among things as the goal of serving God and
doing the commandments. And that is what that perfect
man who truly grasped these ideas, what Antigonus, a
man of Soko, said: Do not be like servants who wait upon
the master with an eye to receiving a gratuity, but be like
servants who wait upon the master with no eye to receiving
a gratuity.[2] With this he wished to say that one should
believe in truth because it is truth. And that is why such
a man is called a servant of love.

And they, blessed be their memory, said: "Happy the
man that feareth the Lord, that delighteth greatly in His
commandments." Said Rabbi Eliezer: For his commandments but not for the reward of doing his commandments.[3]
How clear this is, and what a lucid proof for what has
already been said!

1 Sayings of the Fathers IV. 5.
2 *Ibid.*, 1. 3.
3 Abodah Zarah 19 a, on Ps. 112:1.

And still greater is that which is said in the *Sifre* [1]: Perhaps you will say, See, I shall study the Torah so that I may become a rich man, that I may be called master, that I obtain reward in the coming world; therefore it is taught "to love the Lord thy God": all that you do, you shall do only for love.

And herewith this matter has been made clear to you, and perhaps you also see clearly that this is the purpose of the Torah, and the basis of all that was the goal of our wise men, peace be with them. Only a madman and a fool, whom foolish thoughts and trivial considerations have corrupted and confused, could close his eyes to this. For this also was the rung of Abraham, our father, peace be with him, who was a servant for love; and of this kind shall the arousing be.

But the sages, blessed be their memory, knew very well that this is surpassingly difficult and not every man can grasp it, and that even if he does grasp it, he cannot affirm it at the beginning of his meditations, and is not at all convinced that it can become clear faith. And this is because man does a thing only so that he may have an advantage from it or avoid harm, otherwise he would regard his doing as useless and empty. And how could one say to a learned gentleman: Do this thing, and do not do that, but without fearing punishment from God, blessed be he, and without looking for a good reward? This would be an exceedingly difficult matter, simply because all men do not grasp the truth and are not like Abraham our father—peace be with him!

And so, to give the common people a basis for their faith, they were permitted to do the commandments in the hope of reward, and to refrain from transgressing for fear of punishment. They are spurred on, they are strengthened in their intention, until one of them attains and knows the truth and the nature of the perfect way. One proceeds with them as with the boy who is learning to read, according to the parable I have related. The people certainly do not lose all by doing the commandments for fear of punishment, or in the hope of reward, but they

1 Early Midrash, on Numbers and Deuteronomy.

are imperfect. Yet it is well thus, until they have strength, and have acquired the habit and the ambition of fulfilling the Torah; and thus they are roused to know the truth, and they become servants for love. And that is what they, blessed be their memory, said: A man shall always occupy himself with the Torah and the commandments, even if it is not for their own sake; for even if it is not for their own sake, he will come to do it for their own sake.

THE ROOT OF THE LOVE OF GOD

Eleazar ben Judah

Germany, 12th–13th Century

FROM THE ROKEAH

The soul brims with the love of God. It is bound with the cords of love, is joyful thereat and filled with gladness not like one who serves his master unwillingly, but in such a wise that even if force seeks to prevent it, the heart will burn with the fervent desire to serve, and rejoice to do the will of the Creator, as the singer words it: "Serve the Lord with gladness." And he serves in uprightness, as it is written: "And gladness for the upright in heart." But a man does not serve the Lord for his own profit, and not so that honor may accrue to him. He says: Who am I, "despised and forsaken of men?" Today I am here, tomorrow in the grave. "Behold, I was brought forth in iniquity, and in sin did my mother conceive me." And though I am full of foulness, yet have I been elected and created to serve the King of glory!

For when a man in his very depths thinks upon the fear of God, his heart flames with love, and innermost joy gladdens his soul; great is the rejoicing in him, and wisdom shines from his face. Therefore those who love His name, rejoice in Him. For a man in whose heart there is wisdom of God, fulfills his commandments with a whole heart and in the joy he derives from doing the will of his Creator.

And the lover of God does not consider his profit in this world. He does not concern himself with the pleasures his wife bestows, nor with his sons and daughters. All this is nothing to him, and nothing exists for him save this—to do the will of his Creator, to do kindness to others, to hallow the name of God, and to give himself up to the love of him, as it is written concerning Abraham, "I have lifted up my hand unto the Lord . . . that I will not take a thread nor a shoe-latchet," and like Phinehas, who gave himself up when he slew Zimri. Such men are never overweening. They do not speak idle words; they do not stare at women, and they hear themselves reviled without answering. All their thoughts are with their Creator. They sing psalms to their Maker, and all the substance of their thought burns with love for God. Such a man is blessed in this world and in the world that is to come.

YOU STAND BEFORE THE LORD

Moses Nahmanides

Spain—Palestine, 13th Century

LETTER TO HIS SON

"Hear, my son, the instruction of thy father, and forsake not the teaching of thy mother." Accustom yourself to speak calmly to all men, at all times, and you will save yourself from anger, which is an ill thing that leads man into sin.

And thus spake our teachers, blessed be their memory: Every kind of damnation has power over him who is angry, as it is written: "Remove vexation from thy heart, and put away evil from thy flesh"; but evil means nothing else than the pale of damnation.[1]

And when you have saved yourself from anger, the way of humility will open in your heart, and that is better

1 Nedarim 22 a.

than all good ways, as it is written: "The reward of humility is the fear of the Lord."

And by virtue of humility, the fear of God will rise within your heart, for always will you take to heart "whence you have come, and whither you are bound," [1] and that you are as worms and vermin, even in your life, and how much more in your death, and "in whose presence you will in time give account of yourself and reckoning" [2]— before the King of glory, as it is written: "Behold, heaven and the heaven of heavens cannot contain Thee"; how then the hearts of men! And if you consider all this, you will fear your Creator, and save yourself from sin; and thanks to these ways, you will rejoice in your portion.

And if you constantly accustom yourself to the way of modesty, that you feel humility before every man, and fear God and fear sin, then the Divine Presence [3] will rest upon you with the light of its splendor, and you will live the life in the coming world.

And now, my son, know and see: He who cherishes pride in his heart, and sets himself above all creatures, is a rebel against the kingdom of heaven, for he flaunts the raiment of the Omnipresent, as it is written: "The Lord reigneth; He is clothed in majesty." But of what should the heart of man be proud? Of riches? "The Lord maketh poor, and maketh rich." Of honors? Do they not belong to God? As it is written, "Both riches and honor come of Thee," and how could he boast of the honor of his Maker? Would he boast of wisdom? "He removeth away the speech of men of trust, and taketh away the sense of the elders."

And so we find that before God all are equal, for in his wrath he humbles the proud, and if it is his will, he raises the humbled. Therefore, do you humble yourself, and the Omnipresent will raise you up.

Therefore I want to explain to you why you should accustom yourself to the way of humility, to walk in it constantly.

---

1 Sayings of the Fathers III. 1.
2 *Ibid.*
3 In Hebrew, "Shekinah." The word denotes awareness of the Divine Presence among men, the indwelling of God in the world. It is often used as another expression for God.

Say all that you have to say in calmness. Bow your head
and turn your eyes down to the earth, but your heart up
to the heavens. Do not stare a person in the face when you
are speaking to him. In your eyes, every man should be
greater than yourself. If he is a wise or a rich man, it is
your duty to give him honor. But if he is poor and you
are rich and wiser than he, think in your heart that you
may have more guilt than he, and that he may be more
righteous than you, so that when he sins, he does it through
error, but when you sin, you do so intentionally.

In all that you say and do, in your thoughts and at all
times, regard yourself as one standing before the Omnipresent with his Glory over you, for "the whole earth is
full of His Glory."

And always be intent upon reading the Torah, so that
you may translate it into reality. When you rise from your
book, probe into what you have learned, to discover
whether there is in it anything you can translate into
reality. Examine your doing, both morning and evening,
and all your days will be turnings to God.

And at the time of prayer, clear all worldly matters out
of your heart; prepare your heart before God, blessed be
he, purify your senses, and consider your words before you
allow them to leave your mouth.

And in this wise act all the days of your life, in every
single thing, and you will not fall into sin. And then your
words and your deeds and your thoughts will be upright,
your prayer clear and pure and innocent, directed to God,
blessed be he, and accepted by him, as it is written: "Thou
wilt direct their heart, Thou wilt cause Thine ear to
attend."

Read this epistle once a week and do not fail to translate
it into reality and by its aid to follow forever the Divine
Name, so that you may prosper in all your ways. Thus you
will be found worthy of the coming world, which is re-
served for the righteous.

HANINA BEN DOSA, A SERVANT
BEFORE THE KING

from the Talmud and the Midrash

FOOD

Said Rab Judah in the name of Rab:
Always, day by day.
a voice rings out, [1] saying:
The whole world is fed because of the merit of Hanina,
    my son;
but Hanina, my son, finds sufficient a measure of locust
    pods
from Sabbath eve to Sabbath eve.

BREAD

Always, on the day before the Sabbath, his wife was
wont to heat the oven, and—because she was ashamed—to
throw something into it that gave forth steam.
    But for her neighbor she had a bad woman, who said:
"I know she has nothing at all, so why all this pretense?"
And she went and knocked at her door.
    Then Rabbi Hanina's wife was ashamed and went out,
and into the room.
    But a miracle was wrought upon her, and her neighbor
saw the oven full of bread, and the trough full of dough.
    And the neighbor said: "You, you, fetch a shovel, for
your bread is burning."
    And the other said: "That was what I went out to fetch!"

POVERTY

His wife said to him: "How long must we live in want,
in more and more want?"
    He said to her: "What shall we do?"

_____
[1] In Hebrew, "bat kol." The word denotes a heavenly voice that makes
known God's will.

"Pray that you may be given something!"
So he prayed, and there came forth the shape of an arm,
and he was given the foot of a golden table.

But in a dream she saw this: Once the righteous will be
eating at a golden table with three legs, and she and her
husband alone will eat at a table with two legs. She said
to him: "Are you content to have all the world eat at a
table that is whole and perfect, and we alone at a table that
is imperfect?"

He said to her: "What shall we do?"

"Pray that it be taken away from you."

And he prayed and it was taken from him.

FAITH

Once, on a Friday evening, he could see that his daughter
was downcast.

So he said to her: "My daughter, why are you downcast?"

She answered: "I took the vessel with vinegar for the
vessel with oil, and tried to light the lamp for the Sabbath
with it."

He said to her: "My daughter, why should this trouble
you? He who spoke to the oil, and it burned, will speak
to the vinegar, and it will burn."

And they say that it burned and burned the entire day,
until they fetched light from it for the Habdalah.[1]

THE RAIN

Rabbi Hanina ben Dosa was once walking along, and a
rain fell.

He said to Him: "Lord of the world, all the world is at
ease, only Hanina is in distress."

And the rain stopped.

When he reached his house, he said: "Lord of the world,
all the world is in distress, only Hanina is at ease."

And the rain commenced falling again.

[1] Habdalah ("separation") is the benediction pronounced upon wine,
spices, and light, at the conclusion of Sabbaths and festivals.

SIN

They tell of a place in which a hardim [1] lived, who did harm to creatures, and they came and reported it to Rabbi Hanina ben Dosa.

He said to them: "Show me its hole."

So they went and showed him the hole. He put his heel over the opening, and it came out and bit him. But the hardim died.

He took it on his shoulder, carried it to the house of study, and said to them: "See, my sons, it is not the hardim but sin that kills."

And at this time they said: "Woe to the man who meets with a hardim, but woe to the hardim that meets with Rabbi Hanina ben Dosa."

THE RIGHTEOUS AND HIS BEAST

There is a story about Rabbi Hanina ben Dosa's donkey, which robbers stole. They tied him fast in a courtyard, and set before him straw, oats, and water, yet he neither ate nor drank.

They said: "Why should we hold on to him? That he die and fill our yard with his stench?"

So they went and opened the door and let him out. And he trotted and trotted until he arrived at Rabbi Hanina ben Dosa's. And when he got there, the rabbi's son heard a voice and said: "Father, this voice sounds like the voice of our beast."

The rabbi said: "My son, open the door for him, for he is hungry unto death."

He went and opened the door, and put out straw, and oats, and water for him; and he ate and drank.

And because of this it was said: As the first righteous men were devout, so also their beasts were devout, just as they.

EFFECTUAL PRAYER

This is a story about Rabbi Hanina ben Dosa, who went to study the Torah with Rabbi Johanan ben Zakkai. And

[1] A species of large lizard.

Rabbi Johanan ben Zakkai had a son who fell ill, and so he said: "Hanina, pray for my son, that he may live."

And Rabbi Hanina ben Dosa bowed his head between his knees and prayed for the son, and he lived.

Rabbi Johanan ben Zakkai said: "If ben Zakkai had held his head bowed between his knees all day, his prayer would not have been answered."

His wife said to him: "Why? Is Hanina greater than you?"

He replied: "No, but he is a servant before the king, while I am the prince before the king." [1]

DIGNITY OF CREATURES

This is a story about Rabbi Hanina ben Dosa. He saw a lion and said to him: "Woe to you, weak king! Have I not conjured you not to let yourself be seen in the land of Israel?"

And instantly the lion fled. Then Rabbi Hanina ran after him and said to him: "I beg your pardon! I called you weak king, but He who created you has called you the strong."

THE END

When Rabbi Hanina ben Dosa died, that was the end of men of true deed.

SUSIA OF HANIPOL, THE SAINT

Hasidic Legends

18th–19th Century

THE WORD

Rabbi Israel of Rizin related: All the pupils of my ancestor, of the Great Maggid,[2] transmitted the teachings in

---

1 A servant comes and goes in the house without special permission; a prince has to wait for the king's summons.

2 Dob Baer of Meseritsh (18th century), important follower of Rabbi Israel Baal Shem, and popular preacher (maggid).

his name, all save only Rabbi Susia. And the reason for this was that Rabbi Susia hardly ever heard his teacher's speech to the end. For at the very outset, when the maggid recited the verse from the Scriptures that he was about to expound, and began with the words of the Scripture, "And God said," or "And God spoke," Rabbi Susia was seized with ecstasy, and screamed and gestured so wildly that he disturbed the peace of the table and had to be led out. And then he stood in the hall or in the woodshed, beat his hands against the walls, and cried aloud: "And God said!" He grew quiet only when my ancestor had finished expounding the Scriptures. That is why he did not know the words of the Maggid. But the truth is, I say to you—I say to you the truth is: If a man speaks in the spirit of truth and listens in the spirit of truth, then one word suffices: for with one word can the world be uplifted, and with one word can the world be redeemed.

ONLY THE GOOD

Once the young Susia was in the house of his teacher, the great Rabbi Baer, when a man came before the rabbi and begged him to advise and assist him in an enterprise. But since Susia saw that this man was full of sin and untouched by any breath of repentance, he grew angry, and spoke harshly to him, saying: "How can a man such as you, who have committed this crime and that, have the temerity to stand before a holy countenance without shame or the longing to atone?"

The man left in silence, but Susia regretted what he had said, and did not know what to do. Then his teacher blessed him, so that henceforth he might see only the good in people, even if a person sinned before his very eyes.

But since the gift of second sight accorded to Susia could not be taken from him through words spoken by a man, it came to pass that from this hour on he felt the sins of the people he met as his own, and put upon himself the blame for them.

Whenever the Rabbi of Rizin told this about Rabbi Susia, he was wont to add: And if we were all of like char-

acter, evil would by now be destroyed, and death overcome, and perfection achieved.

SUSIA AND THE SINNER

Once Rabbi Susia came into an inn, and on the forehead
of the innkeeper he saw long years of sin. For a while he
was silent and motionless. But when he was alone in the
room that had been assigned to him, the shudder of vicari-
ous experience came upon him in the midst of singing
psalms, and he cried aloud: "Susia, Susia, you wicked man,
what have you done? There is no lie that has failed to
tempt you, and no crime you have not tasted of. Susia,
foolish, erring man, how will it end with you?" And he
enumerated the sins of the innkeeper—naming the time
and place of each—as his own, and sobbed.

The innkeeper had quietly followed this strange man.
He stood at the door and heard him. First he was stricken
with dull dismay, but then penitence and grace were
lighted within him, and he woke to God.

SUSIA AND THE BIRDS

Once Rabbi Susia journeyed across the country and collected money to ransom prisoners. And he came to an inn,
at a time when the innkeeper was not at home. When,
according to his custom, he went through the rooms, he
saw in one a large cage with all sorts of birds. And Susia
saw that the caged creatures longed to fly in the spaces of
the world, and to be free birds again. He burned with pity
for them and said to himself: "Here you are walking your
feet off, Susia, to ransom prisoners, and what greater ran-
soming of prisoners can there be than to liberate these
birds from their prison?" Upon this he opened the cage
and the birds flew out into freedom.

When the innkeeper returned and saw the empty cage,
he asked the people in the house with great wrath who had
done this to him. They answered: "There is a man loiter-
ing about here, and he looks like a fool, and none but he
can have done this bad thing."

The innkeeper shouted at Susia: "You fool, how could

you have the insolence to rob me of my birds, and to make
worthless the good money I paid for them?"

Susia replied: "You have often read in the psalms, and
repeated: 'His tender mercies are over all His works.' "

Whereupon the innkeeper beat him until his hand was
tired, and finally threw him out of the house. And Susia
went his way serenely.

OF ADAM

Susia once asked his brother, the wise Rabbi Elimelek:
"Dear brother, we read in the Scriptures that the souls of
all men were comprised in Adam. And so we too must have
been there when he ate the apple. I do not understand
how I could have let him eat it! How you could have let
him eat it?"

Elimelek replied: "We had to, we all had to. For had
he not eaten, the poison of the snake would have remained within him for all eternity. Eternally he would
have mused: 'All I need do is to eat of this tree, and I
shall be as God—all I need do is to eat of this tree, and
I shall be as God.' "

HIS DAYS

Every morning, when Rabbi Susia rose, before he spoke
a word to God or to men, it was his custom to call out:
"Good morning to all of Israel!"

In the course of the day, he wrote everything he did on
a slip of paper. Before going to bed in the evening, he
fetched it out, read it, and wept until the writing was
blurred with tears.

DEVOTION

Susia was once a guest in the house of the Rabbi of Neshiz.
And when midnight had passed, the host heard sounds
coming from his guest's room, and he went to the door and
listened. And he heard Susia running up and down in the
room and saying: "Lord of the world, behold! I love you,
but what is there for me to do? I know nothing at all!"

And then he began running up and down again and repeating the same thing, until suddenly he bethought himself and cried: "Why, I know how to whistle, so I shall
whistle something for you."

But when he started whistling, the Rabbi of Neshiz grew
frightened.

THE FEAR OF GOD

Once Susia prayed to God: "Lord, I love you so much,
but I do not fear you enough! Lord, I love you so
much, but I do not fear you enough! Let me stand in awe
of you as one of your angels, who are penetrated by your
awe-filled name."

And God heard his prayer, and his name penetrated the
hidden heart of Susia, as it comes to pass with the angels.
But at that Susia crawled under the bed like a little dog,
and animal fear shook him until he howled: "Lord, let
me love you like Susia again!"

And God heard him this time also.

AT THE CROSSROADS

It came to pass that once when Rabbi Susia was wandering
through the countryside, he came to a crossroads and did
not know which of two roads to take. Then he lifted his
eyes and saw the Glory of God leading the way.

THE END

Rabbi Susia grew very old. For seven years before he died,
he lay on his sickbed, for—so it is said of him—he had taken
suffering upon himself to atone for Israel.

On his tombstone are the words: "One who served God
with love, who rejoiced in suffering, who wrested many
from iniquity."

THE DEATH THROUGH THE KISS OF GOD

Moses Maimonides

Spain—Egypt, 12th Century

FROM MOREH NEBUKIM

The philosophers long have taught that the forces of a young body are an impediment to most of the ethical virtues, and in particular to that pure reflection which man develops from perfect knowledge, which leads to the love of God, and which he cannot possibly develop out of the glowing sap of his body. The more the powers of the body subside and the fires of passion ebb, the stronger the spirit becomes, the brighter its radiance, the purer its knowledge, and the greater its joy over what it knows. When the perfect man grows old and approaches death, this knowledge increases by leaps and bounds, and his happiness over his knowledge, and his love for what he has come to know, are heightened and intensified until his soul departs from his body at the moment of greatest delight.

The sages had this in mind when, concerning the death of Moses, Aaron, and Miriam, they said that these three died through the kiss of God. They explain: It is written: "So Moses, the servant of the Lord, died there in the land of Moab, through His mouth"; this teaches us that he died through the kiss. Likewise is it written of Aaron: "He went up into Mount Hor . . . by the mouth of the Lord, and died there." They also said of Miriam that she died by the kiss, but in her case they do not mention the words "by the mouth of the Lord," because she was a woman and so this figure of speech would be unbeautiful.[1] What it all means, however, is that these three died in the delights of knowledge, died of love that was all too great. With these words the sages, blessed be their memory, imitated the well-known poetic form of expression according to which knowledge, springing from the power of love of God, is

[1] Baba Batra 17 a.

called "kiss"; as it is written: "Let him kiss me with the kisses of his mouth."

The sages, blessed be their memory, mention this form of death, which is actually true liberation from death, only in the cases of Moses, Aaron, and Miriam. The other prophets and pious men were not on a par with these, but the knowledge of all was heightened in death, as it is written: "Thy righteousness shall go before thee; the glory of the Lord shall be thy rearward." This knowledge remains the same through all eternity, for the hindrance that once separated man from what was to be known, is removed. And he continues in a state of high delight, which is not of the nature of bodily delight, as we in our work, and as others before us, have explained.

THE WAYS OF LIFE

FREEDOM OF WILL

Moses Maimonides

Spain—Egypt, 12th Century

FROM MISHNEH TORAH

Man has been given free will: if he wishes to turn toward the good way and to be righteous, the power is in his own hands; if he wishes to turn toward the evil way and to be wicked, the power is likewise in his own hands. Thus it is written in the Torah: "And the Lord God said, Behold, the man is become as one of us, to know good and evil." This means that in regard to this matter, the species of man became single of its kind in this world, and that no other species is like it. Man knows good and evil out of himself, out of his intelligence and reason. He does what he wishes to do, and there is none to restrain his hand from doing either good or evil. And because this is so, he could even "put forth his hand, and take also of the tree of life, and eat, and live for ever."

Do not open your mind to what the fools among peoples of the world and most of the untutored in Israel say, namely, that the Holy One, blessed be he, determines, even at the very creation of every man, whether he shall be righteous or wicked. It is not thus. For indeed every man can become a righteous man like Moses our master, or wicked like Jeroboam, he can be wise or foolish, merciful or cruel, base or noble, and so on in regard to all quali-

ties. But there is none who forces him, none who determines him, none who draws him toward the one or the
other of the two ways. It is he himself who, out of his own
volition, turns to the path he wishes to take. That is what
Jeremiah said: "Out of the mouth of the Most High pro-
ceedeth not evil and good." What he means is that the
Creator does not determine whether a man is to become
good or evil.

And since this is so, it must be concluded that he who
sins does harm unto himself alone. And so it is quite right
that he should weep and lament his sins and that which
he has done to his soul in doing evil. And therefore it is
written: "Wherefore doth a living man complain? Because
of his sins!" Furthermore, because we have the power over
our actions in our own hands and have done this evil,
knowing what we were doing, it is right that we should
turn about and forsake our wickedness, just because the
power is in our own hands. About this it is written: "Let
us search and try our ways, and return to the Lord." This
is a mighty root and pillar of the Torah and of the commandments—as it is said: "See, I have set before thee this
day life and good, and death and evil." And it is written:
"Behold, I set before you this day a blessing and a curse."
This means that the power is in your hands and that everything a man may do of the actions that men do. he will do,
whether it be good or evil. And so it is said: "Oh that they
had such a heart as this alway, to fear Me, and keep all My
commandments." This means: The Creator does not compel man, he does not determine him to do good or evil,
but he leaves it all to him.

If God determined whether a man were to be righteous
or wicked, or if there were something inherent in man that
inexorably drew him to one way among many ways, to a
particular kind of knowledge, to a particular view, to
a particular deed—as foolish astrologers have conceived in
their own fancy—why then did the prophets bid us: Do
this and do not do that! Mend your ways and leave off
transgressing! Why would they say this if, from the moment of his creation, everything about man were deter-

mined, or if his inner law forced him to something from
which he could not withdraw? What reason would there
then be for the entire Torah? And by what right would
God punish the wicked and reward the righteous? "Shall
not the Judge of all the earth do justly?"

And do not be astonished and say: How is it possible
that man should do as he pleases, or that what he does is
left entirely to him; can anything in the world be done
save through the permission of its Master, and against his
will? For the Scriptures say: "Whatsoever the Lord pleased,
that hath He done, in heaven and in earth." But be ad-
vised that all is done according to his will, even if our
actions are left to us ourselves. How this can be? Just as
it is the will of the Creator that fire and air rise but that
water and earth sink down, and that the wheel turns
around and around, and that the other creatures in the
world are according to their fashion as it was his will, so
also he wished man to have the power over his actions in
his own hands, and that what he does be left to him, and
that none compel him or draw him this way or that. Out
of himself and with the knowledge that God has given
him, he is to do all those things which man can do. And
that is why he can be judged according to his doing: if he
has done what is good, all shall be well with him, and if
he has done what is evil, all shall be ill with him. It is this
the prophet says in the words: "This hath been of your
doing"; "They have chosen their own ways." And about
this, Solomon said: "Rejoice, O young man, in thy youth
. . . but know thou, that for all these things God will
bring thee into judgment." This means: Know that the
power to do is in your own hands, but that at some future
time you will be called to account.

Perhaps you will say: The Holy One, blessed be he,
knows all that will come to pass before it has come to pass.
And so, does he or does he not know if a man will be
righteous or wicked? If he knows that a certain man will
be righteous, it is not well possible that this man will
not be righteous. But if you say that he does know a man
will be righteous, and that it is still possible for this man

to become wicked, why then he does not know for certain? Know that the reply to this question is "longer than the earth and broader than the sea," and many mighty roots and many mountains hang thereby. But you must know and understand what I am about to tell you: The Holy One, blessed be he, does not know with a knowledge that is outside of him, as men who are not one with their knowledge. In the case of God, blessed be he, name and knowledge are one and the same thing. The knowledge of man cannot grasp this quite fully; and just as man has not the power to discover and to grasp the truth of the Creator —for it is said, "Thou canst not see My face, for man shall not see Me and live"—so man has not the power to discover and to grasp the knowledge of the Creator. That is what the prophet says: "For My thoughts are not your thoughts, neither are your ways My ways." And since this is so, we have not the power to know the nature of the knowledge of the Holy One, blessed be he, his knowledge of all creatures and of their doing. But we do know beyond a doubt that the doing of man is in his own hands, that the Holy One, blessed be he, does not draw him this way or that, or determine him to do thus and so. And we know this not only through what has been handed down to us by religion, but through clear reasoning from the teachings of wisdom. And so it has been said in the spirit of prophecy that man is judged for what he does according to his doing, whether it be good or evil. And this is a principle on which all the words of the prophets depend.

OF THE WAYS OF LIFE

from the Talmud and the Midrash

AFTER THE DESTRUCTION OF THE TEMPLE

Once Rabban Johanan ben Zakkai went forth from Jerusalem; and Rabbi Joshua walked behind him.

When he beheld the sanctuary that had been destroyed, Rabbi Joshua said: "Woe to us, that it has been de-

stroyed! The place where Israel's sins found atonement!"
Then the other said to him: "My son, do not let it grieve
you! We have atonement equal to that other. And what
atonement is that?
Deeds of love,
as it is written: 'For I desire mercy, and not sacrifice.' "

BLOOD

Once a man came to Raba and said to him:
"He who governs the place I live in, bade me: 'Go, and
kill such and such a man, or I shall have you killed.' "
Then Raba said to him:
"Then let him kill you, but you—you shall not kill! Why
do you think your blood is redder? Perhaps the blood of
that other is redder!"

THE CAUSES OF SUFFERING

Raba—others say it was Rab Hisda—said:
When a man sees suffering coming upon him, he shall examine his works;
when he has examined them and found nothing, he shall
seek the cause in neglect of the Torah;
when he has sought and found nothing, his suffering is
surely suffering for love; [1]
as it is written: "For whom the Lord loveth He correcteth."

DISASTER

Our masters taught:
It once came to pass that Hillel the elder was walking his
way when he heard screams from the direction of the
city.
Then he said: "I am sure that they do not come from my
house."
Concerning him, the Scriptures say:
"He shall not be afraid of evil tidings; his heart is stedfast
trusting in the Lord."

[1] Suffering as a sign of God's love.

SUPPOSITIONS

A man shall do good works, not until then shall he beg the
Torah of God.

A man shall do righteous and worthy works, not until then
shall he beg wisdom of God.

A man shall walk the way of humility, not until then shall
he beg understanding of God.

ASCENT

Rabbi Phinehas ben Yair said:

The Torah leads to deliberation, deliberation leads to
zeal, zeal leads to cleanness, cleanness leads to continence, continence leads to purity, purity leads to godliness, godliness leads to humility, humility leads to the
fear of sin, the fear of sin leads to holiness, holiness leads
to the Holy Spirit, the Holy Spirit leads to resurrection;
but among all qualities, piety is the greatest—

as it is written: "Thou spokest in vision to Thy godly
ones!"

Rabbi Joshua ben Levi objected to this, for Rabbi Joshua
ben Levi said: Humility is the greatest among them all—

as it is written: "The spirit of the Lord God is upon me;
because the Lord hath anointed me to bring good tidings
unto the humble."

THE MONUMENTS OF THE RIGHTEOUS

Rabban Simeon ben Gamaliel says: No tombstones are
erected on the graves of the righteous; it is their words
that are their monuments.

THE CROWN OF CREATION

Our masters taught:

Man was created on the eve of the Sabbath [1]—and for what
reason?

So that in case his heart grew proud, one might say to him:
Even the gnat was in creation before you were there!

1 As last in the order of creation.

ARROGANCE

Rab Hisda—others say Mar Ukba—said:
Concerning a man who is arrogant, the Holy One, blessed
   be he, says:
"I and he cannot dwell together in this world."

TO BE WORTHY OF LIFE

Our masters taught:
When Rabbi Eliezer fell ill, his pupils came to visit him.
They said to him:
"Master, teach us the ways of life, so that by following
   them, we may become worthy of life in the coming
   world."
Then he said to them:
"Watch over the honor of your friends;
Keep your children from speculation, and have them sit
   at the feet of scholars; and when you pray, bethink your-
   selves before whose countenance you stand.
Thus will you grow worthy of life in the coming world."

THE SACRIFICE OF ABRAHAM

Abraham ben David ha-Levi

Spain, 15th Century

FROM HA-EMUNAH HA-RAMAH

I do not mean to say that man should abstain from a study
of the sciences, and surely not of those sciences which lead
him to a knowledge of God, blessed be he. That would
hardly be commendable. But what I do mean to say is this:
Once a man knows of a certainty that there was a revelation of a kind indisputably establishing the reality of divine providence over all creatures, once the prophecy of
the prophet sent by God is substantiated for him by virtue
of the great miracles performed by that prophet, such as
his liberation of his people through the prowess he demon-

strated for them—realizing that this prophet did not offer
anything unacceptable to reason, nor enjoin a law that
one could not observe, and seeing that nothing blameworthy was ever detected in his conduct, and that he did
not ever cease to be extolled and honored before his people
by God, blessed be he—now, if that prophet says to the
nation, God commands this and that and prohibits this
and that, and a man without knowing the reason or the
basis for these commandments and these prohibitions
nevertheless accepts all this on faith and in trust, that one
is a believer. But whoever seeks to feign wisdom and says,
What advantage was there in forbidding them the flesh of
animals that have no cloven hoofs and that do not chew
the cud, or fish that have no fins and no scales, and other
similar things?—such a man does not display the conduct
of one who would incur martyrdom for the fulfillment of
the commandments of God. When these loose their tongues
in such reproofs, we have but one answer to give to them:
that they consider what Abraham our father, peace with
him, did, for that is something even they cannot deny—
how God, blessed be he, informed him in a prophecy, "For
in Isaac shall seed be called to thee," and promised him
many precious things and then commanded him to offer
up his son as a sacrifice. Did Abraham feel urged to play
the wise and contentious man and to say: And where are
those great promises and those great hopes of which you
assured me? No! He gave himself over completely to the
fulfillment of His command and believed that his knowledge was of no merit compared with that of God, and so
he went forth obedient to the command of God, blessed be
he. This attitude of Abraham's was not hidden from God,
blessed be he, but he wanted Abraham's conduct and the
qualities he demonstrated to serve as an example to be
followed by those who would obey God, and as a model
they might set before their eyes.

MAN'S INTENT

Joseph Karo

Spain—Palestine, 16th Century

FROM THE SHULHAN ARUK

If a man cannot learn without sleeping at noon, then let him sleep. But not too long, for it is forbidden to sleep by day longer than a horse who sleeps as long as it takes him to draw sixty breaths. And even in so brief a sleep, man shall not be intent upon his pleasure, but upon restoring his body to serve the name of God, blessed be he!

And so shall it be with all that brings enjoyment to man in this world. He should not be intent upon pleasure, but upon the service of the Creator, blessed be he! As it is written: "In all thy ways acknowledge Him, and He will direct thy paths." And to this our sages add: "Let all your deeds be done for the name of heaven,"[1] so that even optional acts like eating, drinking, walking, sitting, standing, talking—and all the matters requisite for living—shall all be done in the service of the Creator, or of something that leads to serving him.

Thus, if a man is thirsty or hungry, and eats and drinks, intent upon his own pleasure, this is not praiseworthy. Rather shall he eat and drink in the measure needful for life, with the intent of serving his Creator.

And thus shall it also be when he sits in the circle of the upright, or stands in the place where the righteous stand, or goes to the council of worthy men. If he does these things for his pleasure, if he is satisfying his desires or his longings, then it is not praiseworthy, for it is praiseworthy only if he does them in the name of heaven.

And it is the same with sleeping. Needless to say that at a time when he can devote himself to the Torah and to the commandments, he must not indulge in sleep for his comfort! But even if it is the question of a time when he is exhausted and must sleep to rest from his weariness, it is not praiseworthy if he does it for his enjoyment. Rather

[1] Sayings of the Fathers II. 12.

shall he be intent upon giving his eyes sleep and his body
rest, because it is necessary for his health, lest his mind be
confused while devoting himself to the Torah, as a result
of too little sleep.

And it is the same with speaking. Even when he speaks
about things bound up with wisdom, he must be intent
upon serving the Creator, or upon something that leads to
serving him.

Taken all in all: It is the duty of man to turn his eyes
and his heart to his path, and to weigh all his doing in the
balance of reason. If he sees something that will lead to
serving the Creator, blessed be he, let him do it; if not, let
him not do it. Whoever keeps to this, will be constant in
the service of his Creator.

THE PROOF

Hayyim ibn Musa

Spain, 15th Century

FROM MAGEN VA-ROMAH

In my youth I heard a preacher preach about God's being
one and one only, in a speculative manner—in the manner
of philosophers. And he said many times over that if He
were not one only God, then this and that would necessarily follow. Thereupon a man rose, one of those who
"tremble at the word of the Lord," and said: "Misfortune
came upon me and mine at the great disaster in Sevilla.[1]
I was beaten and wounded, until my persecutors desisted
because they thought I was dead. All this have I suffered
for my faith in 'Hear, O Israel: the Lord our God, the
Lord is One.' And here you are, dealing with the traditions
of our fathers in the manner of a speculative philosopher,
and saying: 'If He were not one only God, then this and
that would necessarily follow.' I have greater faith in the

1 Pogrom of 1391.

tradition of our fathers, and I do not want to go on listening to this sermon."

And he left the house of prayer and most of the congregation went with him.

THE FOUNDATION OF DEVOUTNESS

Moses Hayyim Luzatto

Italy—Palestine, 18th Century

FROM THE MESILLAT YESHARIM

The foundation of devoutness, the root of perfect service, is that man clearly sees and finds truly confirmed what his duty is in his world, and on what he should turn his gaze and his striving in all he busies himself with, all the days of his life. For behold, what our sages, blessed be their memory, have taught, is this, that man was created only to delight in the Lord, to rejoice in the glory of his Presence, for that is the true delight, and among all blissful things the most blissful. But the real place for this bliss is the coming world, for it was created for that purpose.

But the path by which we reach this place of our yearning, is the world here. And that is what they said, blessed be their memory: "This world is like an antechamber to the coming world." [1] And the means by which man can reach that goal are the commandments that God has summoned us to do—blessed be his name. And the place where these commandments can be done is this world and only this. That is why man was brought first into this world, namely, that through the means he finds here, he may reach the place prepared for him—and that is the world to come —so that there he may drink of the superabundance of good he has acquired by these means.

And if you further consider it, you will see: True perfection lies only in clinging to Him, blessed be he, and that

[1] Sayings of the Fathers IV. 16.

is what King David said: "The nearness of God is my good"; and he also said: "One thing have I asked of the Lord, that will I seek after: that I may dwell in the house of the Lord all the days of my life." For this alone is good, and whatever else men regard as good is nothing but vanity and a delusion.

But, in order that man may be made worthy of this good, he must first labor and greatly strive to acquire it. And this means that he must strive to cling to Him, blessed be he, with the strength of the works that produce such good, and this—this is doing the commandments.

And behold, the Holy One, blessed be he, has set man in a place where those are numerous who seek to alienate man from him, and these are bodily lusts. If he permits himself to be drawn in their path, he goes farther and farther away from the true good. And so we find that verily he is wedged in the middle of bitter struggle, for all doing in the world, be it for good or for evil, is to try man —poverty on the one side and riches on the other, as Solomon has said, "Lest I be full and deny, and say: 'Who is the Lord?' or lest I be poor, and steal, and profane the name of my God," carefreeness on the one side and suffering on the other, so that man is besieged both before and behind. But if he be steadfast, and win the battle on all sides, then he is the perfect man, regarded as worthy to cling to his Creator; he will issue forth from the antechamber and enter the hall, there to shine in the light of life. And according to the degree to which he has tamed his urges and his lusts, and has removed himself from that which threatens to remove him from the good, and has striven to cling to Him, according to this degree he will attain to it, and delight in it.

And if you go into this matter more deeply, you will see that the world was created for man's use. He, however, stands on a dangerous brink, for if he permits himself to be drawn toward the world, if he moves away from his Creator, behold, he grows corrupt and corrupts the world along with him. But if he governs himself and clings to his Creator, and uses the world only as a tool to help him to serve his Creator, he is lifted up, and the world is lifted with him. For it is uplifting to all creatures that they are the helpers of perfect man, who is hallowed with His holiness, blessed be he.

And behold, they, blessed be their memory, have pointed out to us this basic thought in the Midrash in that they have said: When the Holy One, blessed be he, created Adam, the first man, he took him and led him up to all the trees in the Garden of Eden and said to him: Behold my works, how beautiful they are and how worthy of praise. But all I have created, I have created for your sake. And so direct your spirit to it that you do not corrupt or destroy my world.[1]

And the meaning of the whole is that man was not created because of his place in this world, but because of his place in that to come. His place in this world is nothing but the means for reaching his place in the coming world, for that world is his goal. And you will find many sayings of our sages, blessed be their memory, and all signify the same. They interpret this world as a place and a time for preparation of food, and the world-to-be as a place of rest and enjoyment of that which has been prepared: "This world is like dry land, and the coming world like the sea. If man has not made provision on dry land, whereof shall he eat on the sea?"[2] And there are more of similar examples.

And so you see it is true that never has a man of understanding believed that the goal of the creation of man is his place in this world, for what is the life of man in this world? And is there anyone who really rejoices and is carefree in this world? "The days of our years are threescore years and ten, or even by reason of strength fourscore years; yet is their pride but travail and vanity," made up of every sort of suffering, sickness, pain, and vexation. And after all this comes death. You will not find one man among a thousand to whom the world has rendered his fill of ease and true freedom from care. And even were he to reach the age of a hundred, he would be as if he had died long ago and vanished from the world. And not only this: if the goal of man's creation were contained in this world,

---

[1] Midrash Kohelet Rabbah, on Eccles. 7:13.
[2] *Ibid.*, on Eccles. 7:15.

it would not have been necessary to breathe a soul into him, that precious and lofty soul which is intended to be greater than the Divine Messengers themselves. And how much more so since it finds no satisfaction in the pleasures of this world! And they, blessed be their memory, have taught: In a parable, what is this thing like? Like a burgher who has wed the daughter of a king. Though he may bring her everything in the world, it is worth nothing to her, since she is a king's daughter. Thus the soul: though you bring it all pleasures in the world, they are nothing to it. And why? Because it belongs among higher beings.[1] Therefore they, blessed be their memory, said: "Without your will you are shaped, without your will you were born"[2]; for the soul does not love this world—on the contrary, it holds it in contempt. And if this is so, the Creator, blessed be he, would surely not have made a creature for a goal that is contrary to its kind, and despised by it. No, the creation of man was undertaken for his place in the coming world.

And this is why he was given a soul, for it is good to serve the soul, and it is through the soul that—in the right place, and at the right hour—man receives his reward, one that the soul will not despise as it does this world, but rather one that it loves and desires. How simple this is!

And now, after we know this, we immediately understand the importance of the commandments, and the value of the service that reposes in our hands. For these are the means of bringing us to true perfection, without which nothing can be attained. It is, however, well known that the goal can be reached in no other way than by employing all possible means that serve to attain it. And in proportion to the strength of the means, and the manner in which we make use of them, the goal born out of them, will be. And every slightest deviation in the use of the means will become clearly evident when the goal is reached. This is clear. And from this we may accept it with entire certainty that the care with which the matters of the commandments

1 *Ibid.*, on Eccles. 6:7.
2 Sayings of the Fathers IV. 22.

and the service are tended, must be a very great care, just as those who weigh gold and pearls are extremely careful because of the greatness of their value. And this that is born, will be born in true perfection, will be of everlasting value, above which there is no higher value.

Thus we see that the basic meaning of the life of man in this world is only to keep the commandments, to worship God, and to withstand trials—nothing but this. And the pleasures of this world are there only to be a help to him and a tool, so that he may be tranquil and circumspect, and bend his heart to this service he is in duty bound to perform. And it is right that man turn wholly to the Creator, blessed be he, that he have no other goal in his doing, be it great or small, than to approach him, blessed be he, than to break through any dividing wall that stands between him and his Maker (and everything of material nature is such a wall), until he strives straight toward him, blessed be he, as the iron to the magnet. And let him follow everything of which he can possibly think that it may be a means to this approach, let him seize upon it and not relinquish it. But let him flee, as one flees from fire, all that he thinks might hinder him in this pursuit. As it is said: "My soul cleaves unto Thee; Thy right hand holdeth me fast." For his coming into the world is only for one purpose, to attain this nearness by saving his soul from everything that hinders and harms it.

OPEN THOU MY LIPS

Zechariah Mendel of Jaroslav

Galicia, 18th Century

FROM DARKE ZEDEK

When we talk about evil persons, this may give rise to evil thoughts, and hence, God forbid, to bringing evil into the world. Therefore, let us talk only about the good ways of righteous men, and so bring good into the world.

It is a saying of Rabbi Tarfon's: "I should be surprised if in this generation there were one entitled to utter reproof."[1] For he who does not know in his own soul that he is perfect in righteousness, may not give reproof, since something of evil always clings to him who reproves, and makes it more difficult for him to serve God, blessed be he. As in the case of the hoe with which one digs in filth, and to which filth always clings, so it is with him who reproves without being perfect in righteousness himself.

He does well to consider that the world of the word speaks within him, and that without it, he could not speak —as it is said: "O Lord, open Thou my lips." And a thought could not exist either, unless it were of the world of thought. Man himself is only like the trumpet that produces the tone blown into it; if the blower leaves it, it can produce no sound. And so it is with man if, heaven forbid, God, blessed be he, withdraws from him; for then he can say nothing at all. Let him remember this especially when he is occupied with the Torah or with prayer, and he will be neither arrogant nor boastful.

He does well to fear the word in itself, and to feel shame before it, for the world of the word is comprised within him, as it has just been said: "Open Thou my lips."

All the words a man hears, everything that happens to him, be it love or fear, fame, victory, gratitude, sealing a bond, sovereignty—all occurs only to rouse him to sanctification and to turning to God. Some frivolous act, for instance, that he has perpetrated, even though only a single time, can bring about that he is confronted with a frivolous word in order that he may now repent of what he then committed. And when, in the midst of prayer, reflection about evil seizes upon his thoughts, this occurs in order that now, in his prayer, he may rectify them and uplift them. This is an important maxim for the service of God, blessed be he.

By studying the Torah he can rectify them: if he learns about the love of God, he can rectify the evil he has dis-

[1] Arakin 16 b.

cerned because of that love; if he has been remiss in the
fear of God, he can rectify this when he learns about fear.

It is of fundamental importance to know that heaven
confers upon man the love of God, but that he must rouse
himself to the fear of him. And so he must not be proud
of the love that comes upon him in prayer, for it is not
there through him, but has come upon him from heaven,
from God, blessed be he.

THE ORDER OF THE ESSENES

Flavius Josephus

Palestine—Rome, 1st-2d Century

FROM BELLUM JUDAICUM

Among the Jews there are three different schools of philosophy. The Pharisees constitute the first, the Sadducees the
second, the so-called Essenes,[1] who live according to un-
usually severe rules, the third.

Asceticism and Way of Life. These latter are also Jews
by birth, but among themselves they are united through
love, more than the others. They shun sensual delights as
they shun sin, and they behold virtue in continence and
the bridling of the passions. They do not think well of
marriage, but adopt other people's children while they are
still at a tender age and can be formed, and treat them
as their own, and instill into them their customs of living.
But this does not mean that they wish to do away with
marriage entirely, and with obtaining progeny by way of
marriage.

Community of Goods. They scorn wealth, and are much
to be admired for their community of goods, for there is

[1] The name is probably derived from Aramaic *asa* ("to heal"), or can
mean *hasayya* ("the devout"). The sect existed from about 150 B.C.E.
to the time of the destruction of the Second Temple in 70 C.E.

no one among them who possesses more than another. They have a rule that everyone who wishes to join their sect, must give his fortune over to the whole community; thus throughout neither desperate poverty nor excessive wealth prevails, but all share as brothers in the total fortune, made up of the property of the individual members. They regard oil as foul, and if one of them is anointed against his will, he washes it from his body. For in their eyes a rough skin is just as honorable as always being clad in white robes. The administrators of the joint fortune are chosen by a majority vote, and everyone without exception must be prepared to do service for the good of the community.

Settlements. They have no city of their own, but in every city there are many of them. Members of the order who come from other places have at their disposal all they find among their fellow members, as though it were their own property, and they enter the houses of persons they have never seen as if they were close friends. And that is why they take nothing with them on a journey, save weapons to protect themselves from robbers. In every city there is a special official whose duty it is to take charge of strangers, to supply them with clothing and all else that they need. Their raiment and their entire appearance give the impression that they are boys who are still subject to the master's rod. They do not assume new clothing and shoes until the old fall to pieces or tear with long use. They do not buy and sell among one another, rather does each give the other what he needs, and, vice versa, receive from him what he himself can use. But each can ask any other member of the order for what he needs, even without giving anything in return.

Worship. Their manner of adoring Deity is curious. For before the sun rises they speak no word on mundane matters, and address the star with certain old, traditional prayers, as though they wanted to implore it to rise.

Work. When the sun is up their superiors send them off to that day's work each one is versed in. When they have labored diligently unto the fifth hour,[1] they come

1 Computed from sunrise.

together in a certain place, don a linen cloth, and wash their bodies with cold water.

Dining Hall. After this ablution they go to a special building, which no member of another sect may enter, and here, clean and as though they were crossing the threshold of a sanctuary, they meet in the dining hall. There they seat themselves quietly and calmly, and the baker sets bread before each in turn, while the cook serves each a single course. Before the meal, the priest pronounces a prayer, and no one may eat before the prayer is said. After the meal he prays again, so that at both the beginning and the end, God is honored as the giver of food. Then, after they have removed their garments, which are as it were holy, they go back to their work until dusk. Then they return and dine in the same manner; if visitors happen to be there, these share the meal. Neither loud tones nor any other kind of noise ever desecrates the house, but each lets the other talk in his turn. The silence that prevails in this house gives the impression of an awesome mystery to those who are not within it. But the cause of this quiet is nothing but the unbroken sobriety of the members of the order, who enjoy food and drink only until their hunger and thirst are appeased.

Charity and Studies. The Essenes do nothing save at the express command of their superiors, and in two things alone have they full freedom of action—in giving help to others, and in showing charity. Thus everyone is permitted to come to the aid of those in need of succor, provided they are worthy of it, and to give food to those in want. It is, however, forbidden to make presents to relatives without the consent of the superiors. The Essenes give vent to anger only if it is righteous anger. They are able to control their tempers. Loyalty ranks high with them; and they cultivate peace with great concern. To give their word means more to them than to swear an oath; they even desist from swearing, because they regard it as more reprehensible than perjury. They say that he who cannot obtain belief without calling upon God is already condemned. They have a great preference for studying the writings of the ancients, particularly in order to discover in them what is of benefit to the body and the soul. With the help of these writings they study roots that will banish sickness, and learn to know the properties of stones.

Novices. He who wishes to be taken into this sect is not immediately accepted. First he must live outside the order for a year, in the same way as the members of the order, after they have given him a small hatchet, the above-mentioned loincloth, and a white robe. If, in the course of this year, he passes the test of moderation, he approaches a step nearer to the community: he participates in the cleansing rite of water, but is not yet admitted to the meetings of the order. For after he has given proof of steadfastness, his character is tested for two more years, and only if he appears worthy in this respect also, is he formally received into the order. Before he is permitted to appear at the common meal, he must swear a solemn oath to the members of the order that he will honor God, observe justice toward men, never inflict harm, either of his own volition or at the command of another, that he will always hate the unrighteous and fight the battle of the righteous, and also that he will always act in good faith toward everyone, and especially toward the superiors, because none has office unless God has given it to him. He must also swear that, should he himself ever be in a position of command, he will never abuse his power, nor seek to surpass those subject to him, either in dress or adornments. Furthermore, he obligates himself always to love truth and to expose liars, to keep his hands pure of theft and his soul pure of the taint of unfair profits, to keep nothing secret from the members of the order, and on the other hand never to reveal any of their secrets, even if this mean martyrdom unto death—and, finally, never to communicate the principles of the order to anyone in a way other than that in which he has learned them himself, to spurn highway robbery, to keep secret the books of the sect and the names of the angels. With oaths of this kind, the Essenes make sure of those who newly enter their order.

Exclusion. He who is found guilty of grave sins is excluded from the order, and the man who is thus thrust out often ends in the utmost misery. For he is bound by his oaths and the usage of the order, and so he may accept no food from nonmembers, and lives on herbs, so that his body becomes emaciated and he finally dies as the victim of hunger. Because of this, they have often in compassion taken back one of these unhappy men lying at the point of exhaustion, and accepted the torments that brought him so close to dying as sufficient atonement for his sins.

Law. They are very conscientious and just in making legal decisions. They pronounce judgment only if at least one hundred members are assembled, and there is no appeal from the sentence of the court. After God, the one they honor most is the lawgiver [Moses], and he who blasphemes him is punished with death. They hold it honorable to give obedience to age and the majority. And so if ten of them are together, it is unlikely that one will speak against the opinion of the nine others. Furthermore, they are very careful not to spit before others, or to the right side.

The Sabbath. They are more scrupulous than all other Jews in refraining from work on the Sabbath. As a result, they not only prepare food the day before, in order not to have to light a fire on the Sabbath, but on the day of rest they do not even dare to move a vessel from its place, or to attend to their bodily functions.

Evacuation. On other days they dig out a pit, with the little hatchet, resembling a cleaver, that is handed out to every novice; they spread their cloaks about them in order not to offend the light of God, sit over the pit, and close up the hole with the loose earth. To perform this function they seek out remote places. And even though evacuation of the excrements is something natural, it is usual among them to wash afterward as though they had done something unclean.

Four Classes. According to the length of time they have belonged to the order, they are divided into four classes, and the younger members are, indeed, so inferior to the elder, that these, if they have merely been touched by the younger, wash as if an outsider had made them unclean. They live very long, and many of them grow to be a hundred years old, and it seems to me that this is the result of their simple way of living and of the customs they observe.

Death. And with all this, the most dreadful calamity leaves them cold; for they overcome sorrow by the strength

of their souls, and prefer a glorious death to the longest
life. This attitude of theirs became very evident in the
war against the Romans. They were tortured, their limbs
were racked, burned, broken. They were martyred with
all possible instruments of torture to make them blas-
pheme the lawgiver or to force them to eat forbidden food
—but they did neither the one nor the other. No word of
supplication of their torturers left their lips, and their
eyes remained void of tears. Smiling in the throes of pain,
they mocked their executioners, and they rendered up
their souls joyfully, in the sure hope of receiving them back
again.

THE END-ALL OF KNOWLEDGE

Israel Baal Shem

Podolia, 18th Century

HASIDIC TEACHINGS

"Had they but abandoned Me," says God, "and kept faith
with My Torah!"[1]

This must be interpreted as follows: The end-all of
knowledge is to know that we cannot know anything. But
there are two sorts of not-knowing. The one is the imme-
diate not-knowing, when a man does not even begin to
examine and try to know, because it is impossible to know.
Another, however, examines and seeks, until he comes to
know that one cannot know. And the difference between
these two—to whom may we compare them? To two men
who wish to see the king. The one enters all the chambers
belonging to the king. He rejoices in the king's treasure
rooms and splendid halls, and then he discovers that he
cannot get to know the king. The other tells himself:
"Since it is not possible to get to know the king, we will
not bother to enter, but put up with not knowing."

1 Yerushalmi Hagigah 76 c, interpreting Jer. 16:11.

This leads us to understand what those words of God mean. They have abandoned Me, that is, they have abandoned the search to know me, because it is not possible. But oh, had they but abandoned me with searching and understanding, so keeping faith with my Torah!

Why do we say: "Our God and the God of our fathers?" [1] There are two sorts of persons who believe in God. The one believes because his faith has been handed down to him by his fathers; and his faith is strong. The other has arrived at faith by dint of searching thought. And this is the difference between the two: The first has the advantage that his faith cannot be shaken, no matter how many objections are raised to it, for his faith is firm because he has taken it over from his fathers. But there is a flaw in it: it is a commandment given by man, and it has been learned without thought or reasoning. The advantage of the second man is that he has reached faith through his own power, through much searching and thinking. But his faith too has a flaw: it is easy to shake it by offering contrary evidence. But he who combines both kinds of faith is invulnerable. That is why we say: "Our God," because of our searching, and "the God of our fathers," because of our tradition.

And a like interpretation holds when we say, "The God of Abraham, the God of Isaac, and the God of Jacob," [2] for this means: Isaac and Jacob did not merely take over the tradition of Abraham, but sought out the divine for themselves.

1 Introductory phrase in many prayers.
2 Introductory phrase of the Amidah prayers.

OUT OF THE DEPTHS

THE HERDSMAN WHO COULD
NOT PRAY

Judah he-Hasid

Germany, 12th–13th Century

FROM THE SEFER HASIDIM

There was a certain man who was a herdsman, and he did
not know how to pray. But it was his custom to say every
day: "Lord of the world! It is apparent and known unto
you, that if you had cattle and gave them to me to tend,
though I take wages for tending from all others, from you
I would take nothing, because I love you."

Once a learned man was going his way and came upon
the herdsman, who was praying thus. He said to him:
"Fool, do not pray thus."

The herdsman asked him: "How should I pray?"

Thereupon the learned man taught him the benedictions in order, the recitation of the Shema [1] and the prayer,
so that henceforth he would not say what he was accustomed to say.

After the learned man had gone away, the herdsman forgot all that had been taught him, and did not pray. And
he was even afraid to say what he had been accustomed to
say, since the righteous man had told him not to.

But the learned man had a dream by night, and in it he
heard a voice saying: "If you do not tell him to say what

1 Cf. p. 33, note 1.

he was accustomed to say before you came to him, know that misfortune will overtake you, for you have robbed me of one who belongs to the world to come."

At once the learned man went to the herdsman and said to him: "What prayer are you offering?"

The herdsman answered: "None, for I have forgotten what you taught me, and you forbade me to say: 'If you had cattle.'"

Then the learned man told him what he had dreamed, and added: "Say what you used to say."

Behold, here there is neither Torah nor works, but only this, that there was one who had it in his heart to do good, and he was rewarded for it, as if this were a great thing. For "the Merciful One desires the heart." [1] Therefore, let men think good thoughts, and let these thoughts be turned to the Holy One, blessed be he.

PRAYERS OF THE MASTERS

from the Talmud

Rabbi Eleazar, when he had ended his prayer, spoke thus:
May it be your will, O Lord our God,
to cause to dwell in our lot, love, brotherliness, peace, and
    friendship;
to widen our boundaries through disciples,
to prosper our goal with hope and with future,
to appoint us a share in the Garden of Eden,
to direct us in your world through good companions and
    good impulse;
that we may rise in the morning and find
our heart await to fear your name.

Rabbi Zera, when he had ended his prayer, spoke thus:
May it be your will, O Lord our God,
that we do not sin,

[1] Cf. Sanhedrin 106 b.

so that we fall not into dishonor nor be disgraced before
  our fathers.

Rabbi Hiyya, when he had ended his prayer, spoke thus:
May it be your will, O Lord our God,
that your Torah be our craft,
that our hearts be not overcast,
nor our eyes somber.

Rab Hamnuna, when he had ended his prayer, spoke thus:
May it be your will, O Lord our God,
to place us in a corner where there is light,
and not in a corner where there is darkness,
so that our hearts may not be overcast,
nor our eyes somber.

Rabbi Alexander, when he had ended his prayer, spoke
  thus:
Master of worlds,
it is known and apparent before you
that it is our will to do your will.
But what is hindering us?
The ferment in the dough,[1] and servitude to the kingdoms.
May it be your will to wrest us out of their hands,
so that we may again do the commandments you have
  willed,
with a whole heart.

Raba spoke thus, after he had made his prayer:
My God, before I was formed
I was worth nothing,
and now that I am formed,
it is as though I had not been formed.
Dust I am in life,
and how much more in death!
Here am I, in your presence,
like a vessel filled with shame and disgrace.
May it be your will, O Lord my God,
that I sin no more.

1 The evil urge.

And the sins I have committed,
wipe them away in your great mercy,
but not with suffering and grave sickness.

Mar, the son of Rabina, when he had ended his prayer,
    spoke thus:
My God,
Keep my tongue from evil,
and my lips from speaking guile.
To those who curse me, let my soul be silent,
my soul shall be to all as dust.
Open my heart to your Torah,
let my soul hasten to do your commandments.
And succor me from evil schemes, from evil impulses,
and from evil women,
from all evil that rushes to come into the world.
But as for those who think evil against me,
break their plots and destroy their thoughts.
Let the words of my mouth
and the meditation of my heart
be acceptable in your presence,
O Lord, my rock, my redeemer.

THE SOUL YOU HAVE GIVEN ME

from the Morning Prayer

O Lord, the soul that you have given me is pure!
You created it, you formed and breathed it into me, you
    keep it within me,
In time you will take it from me, and return it to me in
    the life to come.
As long as my soul is within me, I will give thanks to you,
O Lord my God, and the God of my fathers,
master of all deeds, lord of all souls!

GRACE AFTER MEALS

from the Prayer Book

Blessed be you, O Lord our God, king of the world, who in his goodness feeds the whole wide world.
In grace, in mercy, and in kindness, he gives food to all flesh, for his mercy endures for ever.
And because of his great goodness, we have never lacked food, and may we never suffer want of it, for the sake of his great name.
For he feeds and tends the universe; he does good to the world, and provides food for all the creatures he has wrought.
Blessed be you, O Lord, who feed the universe.

FROM DARKNESS TO LIGHT

from the Prayer Book [1]

May it be the will of our Father who is in heaven to establish the house of our life, and to restore his Divine Presence to our midst, speedily in our days; and let us say amen.

May it be the will of our Father who is in heaven to have mercy upon us and upon our remnant, and to keep destruction and the plague from us and from all his people, the house of Israel; and let us say amen.

May it be the will of our Father who is in heaven to preserve among us the wise men of Israel—them, their wives, their sons and daughters, their disciples and the disciples of their disciples, in all the places of their habitation; and let us say amen.

[1] This prayer is recited by the Reader on Mondays and Thursdays, after the reading from the Torah.

May it be the will of our Father who is in heaven that good tidings of salvation and comfort be heard and published, and that he gather our banished ones from the four corners of the earth; and let us say amen.

As for our brethren, the whole house of Israel, such of them as are given over to trouble or captivity, whether they abide on the sea or on the dry land—may the Omnipresent have mercy upon them, and bring them forth from trouble to respite, from darkness to light, and from subjection to redemption, now, speedily and soon; and let us say amen.

THE END OF THE SABBATH [1]

Isaac ben Judah ibn Ghayyat

Spain, 11th Century

Who set apart the sacred and profane,
May He have mercy on our sins, and deign
To multiply our seed and what we gain,
Like sand, like stars by night.

The palm spins out her shadow, day has waned,
I call to God who holds me in his hand,
The watchman said, the morning cometh and
The night—also the night!

Your justice stands like Tabor, yet I pray
My sin may seem to you a yesterday,
A fleeting fault that swiftly ebbs away,
A vigil in the night.

The time when I could supplicate is past,
Ah, that my spirit found repose at last!

[1] A hymn originally written for the Neilah service of the Day of Atonement, now sung at the conclusion of the Habdalah service ending the Sabbath.

My sighs have left me weary and aghast,
I weep through every night.

Accept my plea without severity,
And fling the holy portals wide for me.
My brows are wet with many drops, oh see;
My locks are dewed with night.

Have pity on me, awe-full Lord on high,
And succor me this day, oh hear my cry,
This evening when the sun has left the sky,
In darkness of the night.

I call upon you, God, to help me know
The path of life that you would have me go,
To raise me from my lowly state, to show
Your grace from dawn to night.

Oh, make me clean of my iniquity,
So none may ask, to vex and sadden me,
Where is this God who wrought you? Where is he
Whose word is song by night!

For in your hand we are no more than clay!
Forgive the grave transgression and the slight,
And tidings will speed forth from day to day,
Resound from night to night.

INVOCATION

Kaddish of Levi Isaac of Berditshev

Volhynia, 18th Century

HASIDIC SONG

Good morning to you, Lord of the world!
I, Levi Isaac, son of Sarah of Berditshev, am coming to
    you in a legal matter concerning your people of Israel.
What do you want of Israel?

It is always: Command the children of Israel!
It is always: Speak unto the children of Israel!
Merciful Father! How many peoples are there in the
    world?
Persians, Babylonians, Edomites!
The Russians—what do they say?
    Our emperor is the emperor!
The Germans—what do they say?
    Our kingdom is the kingdom!
The English—what do they say?
    Our kingdom is the kingdom!
But I, Levi Isaac, son of Sarah of Berditshev, say:
    "Glorified and sanctified be His great name!" [1]
And I, Levi Isaac, son of Sarah of Berditshev, say:
I shall not go hence, nor budge from my place
until there be a finish
until there be an end of exile—
"Glorified and sanctified be His great name!"

IN JUDGMENT

from the Burial Service

Blessed be the Lord our God, king of the universe,
who formed you in judgment,
who nourished and sustained you in judgment,
who brought death on you in judgment,
who knows the number of you all in judgment,
and will hereafter restore you to life in judgment.
Blessed are you, O Lord,
who quickens the dead.

[1] Introductory words of the Kaddish prayer.

TURNING TO GOD

SINNING AND TURNING [1]

from the Talmud and the Midrash

SINNERS AND SIN

Profligates frequented the neighborhood where Rabbi
  Meir lived, and tormented him roundly.
And because of this he prayed that they might die.
Whereupon Beruriah, his wife, said to him:
"What are you thinking of?
Is it because it is written: 'Let sins cease out of the earth'?
but does it say 'sinners'?
'Sins' is what is written!
And more than this:
Look below, at the end of the verse: 'And let the wicked
  be no more.'
When sin is consumed, there are no more wicked.
Rather pray for them,
that they may change and turn
and be wicked no more."
And Rabbi Meir prayed for them,
and they changed and turned to God.

YOU YOURSELF

The Holy One, blessed be he, the Lord, who is called
righteous and upright, has not created man "in His own

1 The Hebrew word, *teshubah*, usually translated as "repentance,"
denotes the change in the sinner's heart and actions. i.e., his turning
from the evil way *to* the right way, his "return to God."

image" save in the sense that man be as righteous and upright as he himself.

Perhaps you will ask why the Holy One, blessed be he,
has created the evil urge, of which it is written: "For the
imagination of man's heart is evil from his youth." The
Holy One himself says that it is evil: who then could
render it good?

The Holy One, blessed be he, replies: You yourself are
he who makes it evil. How? A child of five, of six, of seven,
eight, or nine years does not sin. Not until he is ten years
old, does he begin to sin; it is then he raises the evil urge,
so that it grows big.

Perhaps you will say: Man cannot help himself!

The Holy One, blessed be he, answers: There are so
many things in the world that are mightier than the evil
urge and more bitter, and yet you make them sweet. You
will find nothing more bitter than the lupine, but you
take the trouble to boil it in water seven times over, and
to sweeten it until it grows sweet; and so it is with mustard,
and capers, and many other things. If then you sweeten
for your use the bitter things I have created, how much
more you could do this with the evil urge, which was given
into your hand.

IRONWORK

Rabbi Simeon ben Eleazar said: I shall speak to you in a
parable—to what can we compare the evil urge? To iron
that one has put into the glowing fire; while it is in the
glowing fire, one can make utensils from it, anything you
like.

And just so it is with the evil urge: there is no way to
shape it aright, save through the words of the Torah, which
is like fire.

FIRE AND FLESH

Once women prisoners were taken to Nehardea. They were
lodged in the house of Rab Amram the Devout, and the
ladder was taken from under them.

But when one of them passed, a beam of light fell on

the skylights. Thereupon Rab Amram took the ladder—ten men could not lift it, but he lifted it unaided—and climbed up. When he was halfway up the ladder, he stopped and cried in a loud voice: "Fire at Amram's!"

And the masters came and said to him: "We have shamed you."

Whereupon he answered them: "Better that you have shamed Amram in this world, and need not be ashamed of him in the coming world."

Then he conjured the urge to leave him, and it left him in the guise of a pillar of fire. And Amram said to it: "Behold, you are fire, and I am flesh, yet I am mightier than you."

TODAY

Rabbi Eliezer said: "Turn to God the day before you die."

And his disciples asked him: "Does a man know on which day he will die?"

And he answered them, saying: "Just because of this, let him turn to God on this very day, for perhaps he must die on the morrow, and thus it will come about that all his days will be days of turning to God."

THE PLACE OF THOSE WHO TURN TO GOD

Rabbi Abbabu said: In that place where those stand who have turned to God, the perfectly righteous cannot stand, as it is written: "Peace, peace, to him that is far off and to him that is near"—first to him who is far off, and then to him who is near!

THE BUILDING OF THE TEMPLE AND
THE WEDDING FEAST

from the Midrash

Rabbi Ishmael said: The night Solomon finished building the Temple, he took Batiah, Pharaoh's daughter, to wife.

And there were two celebrations, one in honor of the Temple, and one in honor of Pharaoh's daughter.

Then said the Holy One, blessed be he: "Which shall I accept, this or that?"

Then it was that he resolved in his heart to destroy Jerusalem.

Rabbi Hunia said: On that night, Pharaoh's daughter danced eighty different dances.

The masters said: Pharaoh's daughter ordered a thousand musical instruments to be played before him on that night. She said to him: "That is the way they play for this idol, and this is the way for that."

Solomon slept until the fourth hour of the following day. The keys of the Temple lay under the king's pillow.

But the people were sad on this day of the dedication of the Temple, for the morning offering could not be made, since no one dared wake the king.

Then his mother went to him and reproved him. Some say he was reproved by Jeroboam, the son of Nebat.

ELISHA BEN ABUYAH, THE APOSTATE

from the Talmud

THE IMPURE WISH

Abuyah, my father, was one of the great men of Jerusalem. On the day of my circumcision he called together all the great men of Jerusalem and had them sit in a certain room, but Rabbi Eliezer and Rabbi Joshua in another room. After they had eaten and drunk, the men began to clap their hands and dance.

Thereupon Rabbi Eliezer said to Rabbi Joshua: "While they are busy with their concerns, let us busy ourselves with our concerns." And so they sat down and busied themselves with the words of the Torah, and from the Torah they went on to the Prophets, and from the Prophets to the Writings, and a fire descended from heaven and limned them with flame.

And Abuyah said to them: "Gentlemen, have you come to burn my house down over my head?"
They answered him: "God forfend! We were just sitting here and linking together the words of the Torah, the Torah and the Prophets, and the Prophets and the Writings. And the words rejoiced, as at that time when they were uttered on Sinai, and the fire played around them, as it played around them on Sinai, for on Sinai they were given through fire: 'And the mountain burned with fire unto the heart of heaven.'"
Then Abuyah, my father, said to them: "Gentlemen, if the strength of the Torah is so great, let my son, if he lives, be destined for the Torah."
But because this intention of his was not in the name of heaven, it was not realized for me.

THE GARDEN OF MYSTICAL KNOWLEDGE

Four entered the garden. One looked and died. One looked and lost his mind. One looked and hacked down the shoots. One entered in peace and went forth in peace.
Ben Zoma looked and died. Concerning him the Scriptures say: "Precious in the sight of the Lord is the death of His saints."
Ben Azzai looked and lost his mind. Concerning him the Scriptures say: "Hast thou found honey? Eat so much as is sufficient for thee, lest thou be filled therewith, and vomit it."
Aher looked and hacked at the shoots. Who is Aher? Elisha ben Abuyah.
Rabbi Akiba entered in peace and went forth in peace. Concerning him the Scriptures say: "Draw me, we will run after thee; the king hath brought me into his chambers."

FOR RIGHTEOUSNESS

Once Aher was sitting on the plain of Gennesaret and studying. He saw a man climb a date palm and take "the dam sitting upon the young," and come down without harm. The next day he saw another man climb the date palm, take the young, and "let the dam go." But when he came down, a snake bit him and he died.

He said: "It is written, 'Let the dam go, but the young thou mayest take unto thyself; that it may be well with thee, and that thou mayest prolong thy days.' But how did it go well with that man, and how were his days prolonged?"

Some say that he saw the martyred Judah the Baker's tongue in the bloody jaws of a dog. He said: "Such is the Torah, and such is its reward? This is the tongue that uttered the words of the Torah in their order! This is the tongue that labored in behalf of the Torah all its days! Such is the Torah, and such its reward?"

It seems that there is no reward and no resurrection of the dead.

THE APOSTATE

After Aher had fallen prey to evil ways, he asked Rabbi Meir: "What does it mean when it is written, 'Gold and glass cannot equal it; neither shall the exchange thereof be vessels of fine gold'?"

The rabbi said to him: "Those are the words of the Torah, which are as difficult to acquire as that which is made of fine gold, and as easy to destroy as that which is made of crystal."

The other said: "Rabbi Akiba, your teacher, did not say that, but, 'Just as that which is made of gold and crystal can be mended if it be broken, so a wise man can be righted, even if he have grown corrupt.' "

Rabbi Meir replied: "Then turn again!"

The other said: "I have already heard a voice speak behind the curtain of heaven: 'Return, O backsliding children'—all except Aher."

ALIEN FIRES

They told: When Aher entered the house of study and saw boys sitting there with their books, he said: "What are they sitting here for? What are they doing? They could ply trades; this boy could be a mason, that one a carpenter, and that one a tailor."

And when the boys heard this, they left off studying and went away.

What was the matter with Aher? The songs of the Greeks never left his mouth. They said of Aher that when he rose up in the house of study, many heretical books fell from his lap.

TURNING AND DEATH

After a time Elisha fell ill. And they came and said to Rabbi Meir: "Behold, your teacher is ill."

He went to see him, found him ill, and said to him: "Would you not like to turn to God?"

The other asked: "And if I turned, would it be accepted?"

The rabbi answered: "Is it not written, 'Thou turnest man to contrition'—to contrition of the soul, and still he is accepted?"

Then Elisha wept and that selfsame hour he departed and died.

And Rabbi Meir rejoiced in his heart and said: "It seems that the master died right in the midst of turning to God."

THE MEMORY OF THE TORAH

Aher's daughter came before Rabbi Judah the Prince, and said to him: "Master, take care of me!"

He asked her: "Whose daughter are you?"

She replied: "I am Aher's daughter."

He said to her: "So one of his seed is still in the world! It is written: 'He shall have neither son nor son's son among his people!' "

She answered him: "Think of how he studied the Torah, do not think of his doing!"

And a fire came down and charred Rabbi Judah's chair.

Then he wept and said: "If this comes to pass for the sake of those who abuse the Torah, how much more so for those who are proud of the Torah!"

And he gave orders that she be cared for.

THE DOCTRINE OF TURNING

Moses Maimonides

Spain—Egypt, 12th Century

FROM THE MISHNEH TORAH

Which is the perfect turning? When an occasion arises for repeating a transgression once committed, and it is in the sinner's power to sin again, but he makes himself free, and does not do it. He refrains because he has turned to God—not because he is afraid, or because of lack of strength. How? A man has gone to a woman and sinned with her, and after a time they meet alone. And his love for her persists, and the strength of his body is as it was, and he is at the very place where he has sinned, yet now he makes himself free, and does not sin: that is the perfect turning. It is this that Solomon said: "Remember then thy Creator in the days of thy youth."

But if a man does not turn until he has come into old age, if he turns at a time when it is no longer possible for him to do as he was wont: although this is not a perfect turning, still it will help him and he still is one who has turned to God. Even if he has sinned all the days of his life, yet turns on the day of his death, and dies as one who has turned to God, all his transgressions will be forgiven. For it is written: "Before the sun, and the light, and the moon, and the stars are darkened, and the clouds return after the rain," and that is the day of death. Therefore, if he has remembered his Creator, and turned to him before death, he is forgiven.

And what is turning? It is this—that the sinner relinquishes his sin, that he purges it from his thought, and resolves in his heart to do it no more. As it is written: "Let the wicked forsake his way, and the man of iniquity his thoughts; and let him return unto the Lord, and He will have compassion upon him, and to our God, for He will abundantly pardon." And so he should repent of the past, as it is written: "Surely after that I was turned, I repented," and He who knows hidden things, testifies for him that never in the days to come will he return to this sin, as it is written: "Neither will we call any more the work of our hands our gods."

And he must profess with his lips and utter those resolutions that he has made in his heart.

But he who professes in words and has not resolved in his heart that he will leave off sinning, is like one who goes to the bath of purification with vermin in his hands. For the bath will not benefit him until he has cast away the vermin. And so it is written: "Whoso confesseth and forsaketh them shall obtain mercy." And he must reveal his sin in detail, as it is written: "Oh, this people have sinned a great sin, and have made them a god of gold."

One of the ways of turning is that he who turns constantly cries aloud to God, in tears and supplication, and that he does good according to his powers, and removes himself far from the matter wherein he sinned. And he should also change his name, as if to say: "I am another, and not the man who has committed that deed." He should change all his deeds, so that they be directed to goodness and the straight path; and he should exile himself from his city, for exile atones for sin, since it gives him the opportunity to subject himself, to be humble and bowed in spirit.

And it will accrue to the high praise of whosoever turns to God, if he confesses before many, makes known to them his transgressions, reveals the transgressions he has committed against his neighbor, and says to them: "Of a truth I have sinned . . . and thus and thus have I done," and now, on this day, do I turn and repent. But he who is haughty and reveals not but hides his transgressions, his turning is imperfect, as it is written: "He that covereth his transgressions shall not prosper."

About what has all this been written? About transgressions occurring in the relationship between man and man.

But those transgressions which have to do with the relationship between man and God—concerning those he need say nothing at all, and to reveal them is a shameless act. Rather, let him turn before God, blessed be he, and list his sins before him one by one; but before the many let him confess them as a whole. And it is desirable for him that his transgression be not made known, as it is written: "Happy is he whose transgression is forgiven, whose sin is covered."

Although it is right at any time to turn to God and to cry out, in the ten days between the New Year and the Day of Atonement it is even more right, and it is instantly accepted, as it is written: "Seek ye the Lord while He may be found." About what were these words said? About an individual—but whenever the congregation turn and cry aloud with all their hearts, answer is given, as it is written: ". . . God so nigh unto them, as the Lord our God is whensoever we call upon Him."

But turning to God, and the Day of Atonement, atone only for those transgressions committed in the relationship between man and God—for instance, when a man has eaten forbidden food, or entered into a forbidden marriage, or the like. But in regard to the transgressions occurring in the relationship between man and man—if, for example, he has injured his neighbor, or cursed him, or robbed him, or the like—he will never find forgiveness until he has rendered back to his neighbor what he owes him, and has begged forgiveness of him.

Even though he has returned what monies he owed him, he must still pacify him, and beg forgiveness of him. And if he has hurt his neighbor with words only, he must pacify him, and implore him until he grant forgiveness. But if his neighbor refuses to forgive, let him send a deputation of three men from among his friends to urge him and plead with him. And if he still refuses, a second and a third deputation must be sent. If his neighbor persists in his obduracy, he shall leave him and go his ways, and in that case he who refuses to forgive becomes the sinner. But if a man has transgressed against his teacher, he must go and come, and come and go, even a thousand times, until he obtain forgiveness.

It is forbidden to man to be cruel and unforgiving. It should be easy to evoke his willingness to forgive and difficult to arouse his wrath, and when a transgressor begs forgiveness, at that same hour let him forgive with all his heart and with a willing soul. Even though the transgressor was his enemy, and did him much wrong, let him not avenge the wrong, or bear a grudge. For this is the way of Israel's seed and of their upright hearts.

But if a man has sinned against his neighbor, and the neighbor dies before he has asked his forgiveness, then let the transgressor bring ten men, bid them stand at his neighbor's grave, and say in their presence: " 'I have sinned against the Lord, the God of Israel,' and against him who lies here, for I have done thus and thus to him." If it was money he owed him, let him repay it to his heirs; if he does not know the heirs, let him deposit it in the court of justice, and make his confession.

WORSE THAN SIN

a Hasidic Interpretation

"The Lord! The Lord!" That means: I am one and the same merciful God before a man sins and after he sins.[1]

Maharsha [2] of blessed memory raised the question: What need does a man have of mercy before he sins?

There is, however, an account in the book *Duties of the Heart*,[3] of a certain righteous man who said to his disciples: If there were no sin in you, I would have fear in your be-

1 Rosh ha-Shanah 17 a.
2 Rabbi Samuel Eliezer Edels (1555–1631, Poland), an important expounder of the Talmud.
3 Hobot ha-Lebabot, Gate of Return, chap. 8.   Cf. Index under Bahya ibn Pakuda.

half of something that is worse than sin, and that is pride. For he who believes that he has not sinned, has pride within himself, and that is worse than sin. And thus before a man sins he is certainly in need of mercy to gain forgiveness for the pride in his heart.

ON PRIDE AND ON THE NATURE OF EVIL

Israel Baal Shem

Podolia, 18th Century

"These are the words which Moses spoke unto all Israel beyond the Jordan, in the wilderness."

Many a man who believes God is close to him, knows not of him. But he is close to many a man who yearns for him from afar. Now you are always to think you are standing on the shore of the Jordan and have not as yet entered the Promised Land. And even though you have done all manner of commandments—you have done nothing.

Pride is more heinous than all sin. Because these words of God—concerning himself—hold for all the sinful: ". . . Who dwelleth with them in the midst of their uncleannesses." But our sages teach that, concerning the arrogant, God says: "I and he cannot dwell together in this world."[1]

In the story of creation we read: "And behold, it was very good." But when Moses spoke to Israel to remind them, he said: "See, I have set before thee this day life and good, and death and evil."

Whence did evil come?

Evil too is good, but it is the very lowest rung of perfect good. If one does the good, then evil also becomes good; but if one sins, then it really becomes evil.

[1] Sota 5 a.

MESSENGERS

Nahman of Bratzlav

Ukraine, 18th–19th Century

Man can serve God with the evil urge, provided he directs its flames and greedy fire to God. And without the evil urge, there can be no perfect service.

If a man does not judge himself, all things will judge him, and all things will become the messengers of God.

TALES OF THE TURNING

Hasidic Legends

18th–19th Century

THE GREAT TRANSGRESSION

Rabbi Bunam said to his Hasidim: Man's great transgression is not the sins that he commits—temptation is strong and his power is slight! Man's great transgression is that at every instant he could turn to God—and that he does not turn.

ETERNAL BEGINNINGS

A student asked the rabbi of Berditshev: "The Talmud teaches that 'those who are perfectly righteous cannot stand in that place where those stand who turn to God.' [1] According to this, one who has been stainless from youth on comes after one who has transgressed against God many times, and cannot attain to his rung?"

The zaddik replied: "Whosoever sees a new light every day, light that he did not see the day before, he—if he wishes truly to serve—must condemn his imperfect service of yes-

[1] Berakot 34 b.

terday, atone for it, and begin anew. But the stainless one, who believes he has done perfect service, and persists in it, does not accept the light, and comes after him who everlastingly turns anew."

IN THE PULPIT

When Rabbi Ezekiel, the son of the rabbi of Zans, was stopping in Ujhely, a city in Hungary, he bade it be proclaimed that he would preach in the house of prayer. At the time set, the entire congregation gathered. The rabbi ascended the pulpit and said: "Gentlemen, listen to me! Once I delivered a sermon in this place, and my intention was divided, and not wholly turned to heaven. But to preach with divided purpose is a great sin. And so I resolved to do penance. Since, however, according to the words of our wise men, a wrong must be expiated in the place where it was done, I have again come to this pulpit. And so I implore holy God, praise be to him, to forgive me."

At this, the entire congregation grew aware of the power of God's word, their hearts were seized with the fear of God, and they all turned to him.

THE PENITENT WHO WAS ASHAMED

A sinner who wanted to atone came to the rabbi of Ropshitz to find out what he was to do. He was ashamed to confess all his sins to the zaddik, and yet he was obliged to reveal every one of them, in order to learn what penance he was to perform. And so he said that one of his friends had committed these sins, but had been too ashamed to come in his own person, and had commissioned him to inquire what purification was necessary for each sin.

Smilingly Rabbi Naphtali looked into the cunning, tense face before him. "Your friend," he said, "is a fool. He might well have come in his own person and pretended to me that he was taking the place of another who was ashamed to come himself."

THE GAMBLERS

A Hasid complained to Rabbi Wolf that certain persons were turning their nights into days, playing cards. "That is good," said the zaddik. "Like all men, they too wish to serve God, and do not know how. But now they are learning to stay awake and to persevere in doing something. When they have become perfect in this, all they have left to do is to turn to God—and oh, what servants they will then make for God!"

SERMON ON THE DAY OF ATONEMENT

Isaac Meir of Ger

Poland, 19th Century

On the Day of Atonement the rabbi of Ger spoke to the Hasidim gathered around his table:

"Our teacher Hillel says: 'If I am not for myself, who is for me?' [1] If I do not perform my service, who will perform it for me? Everyone must perform his own service. And then he says: 'And if not now, when?' When will the "now" be? The now that is now, the moment in which we are speaking, has never existed, from the time when the world was created, and will never again exist. Formerly there was another now, and later there will be another now, and every now has its own particular service; as it is written in the holy book Zohar: 'The raiment of morning is not the raiment of evening.'

"Let each labor and strive for the Torah with all his might, and he will become bound up with the Torah. But the sixty myriad souls of Israel of which the Torah speaks, correspond to the sixty myriad letters of the Torah—and so each becomes related to the whole. And if one becomes part of the whole, one receives from the whole—one receives even more than one puts into it. And in this way, a man, in addition to his own now, may receive of the

1 Sayings of the Fathers I. 14.

now of another, of the good he is accomplishing in this now. And again our teacher Hillel says: 'If I am for myself alone, what am I?' Should I, God forbid, be separated from the community, when shall I be able to compensate for my now? For no other now can compensate for this present now, since every moment is limned in its own particular light.

"Whosoever talks about and reflects upon an evil thing he has done, is thinking the vileness he has perpetrated, and what one thinks, therein is one caught—with one's whole soul one is caught utterly in what one thinks, and so he is still caught in vileness. And he will surely not be able to turn, for his spirit will coarsen and his heart rot, and besides this, a sad mood may come upon him. What would you? Stir filth this way or that, and it is still filth. To have sinned or not to have sinned—what does it profit us in heaven? In the time I am brooding on this, I could be stringing pearls for the joy of heaven. That is why it is written: 'Depart from evil, and do good'—turn wholly from evil, do not brood in its wake, and do good. You have done wrong? Then balance it by doing right.

"And so today, the day before the Day of Atonement, we should feel that we are leaving sin and strengthening our hearts, and that we are doing this from the depths of our hearts and not through forced ecstasy, and receiving it with our hearts for all the days to come, and we should rejoice and recite the confession of our sins as quickly as possible, and not dwell upon them, but dwell on the words, 'And you alone will rule, O Lord!' " [1]

THE VOICE FROM HEAVEN

Isaac of Worki

Poland, 19th Century

They asked Rabbi Isaac of Worki how the following saying of our sages should be interpreted: "You shall do all

[1] From the prayers of the New Year and Day of Atonement.

your host tells you, all save going away." [1] For it seems we
certainly ought to obey our host when he bids us go!

The rabbi replied: "Those who believe that the word
'host' here refers to God, are right. We should obey him
in all things, save when he bids us go from him. For we
know that 'he that is banished be not an outcast from him.'
The truth of the matter is that he who has done much evil
must travel a most stormy road in order to turn to God.
For heaven itself tells him that his turning is not wanted
and will not be accepted. But if he does not allow this to
confuse him, if these very tidings rouse his spirit, and he
says, 'All the same,' and turns to God, he will be healed.
We are told that the archheretic Elisha ben Abuyah, who
was called Aher, 'the other,' heard a voice crying from
heaven: ' "Return, O backsliding children"—all except
Aher.' [2] Then he cast off the last ties that bound him to the
law and the community, and renounced truth. Yet God,
by rejecting him, had shown him the only way that leads
to acceptance."

1 Pesahim 86 b.
2 Hagigah 15 a.

PARENTS AND CHILDREN

CONCERNING THE LEARNING
OF CHILDREN

Zevi Hirsh Kaidanower

Lithuania—Germany, 17th–18th Century

FROM KAB HA-YASHAR

Our masters, blessed be their memory, said that the world
endures only for the sake of the breath out of the mouths
of children who go to school.[1] From this you see that great
is the reward of those who teach children. And in every
place where children are learning from a wise man, in that
place dwells the Divine Presence. There is a passage in
the Zohar, in the portion "Go thou": When Rabbi Simeon
ben Yohai came and wanted to see the boys in school, he
said: "I am going to gain sight of the Divine Presence."
But the fact that this is emphasized, and it says, "When he
came and wanted to see the boys in school," is because
this was the custom among men of saintliness. When
they were free from work, they went to the teachers to gain
sight of the Divine Presence. And that is why a man must
be careful, for whoever enters the house of a teacher will
find there "the mother"—that is, the Divine Presence—
"sitting upon the young"; the wings of the Presence are
spread over the little lambs. But the breath from the mouth
of a child can split the vault of heaven and the firmament.
And so the teacher should take to heart that the Divine

[1] Shabbat 119 b.

Presence dwells beside him, and perform his work faithfully, and without falseness, for it is a work of heaven. And he shall see to it that the room in which the children learn, is clean, unspotted with any kind of soilure, and make real the words, "Therefore shall thy camp be holy," for it is the camp of the Divine Presence.

And when the time has come for the child to go to school, so that he may study with a teacher, the father should rise early in the morning and take the child, so that he himself may bring it to the house of the teacher. Whether the father be an old man or a great man, an elder or a master, he must not be ashamed to take his son to school this first time, but rather give praise and thanks to the Holy One, blessed be he, for according him the grace to accord his son grace by placing him "under the wings of the Divine Presence." And on this errand, the mother or the father has the duty of shielding the child with a mantle, so that nothing unclean in the world can lay eyes upon it. And when the father has brought the child to school, he should place it in the teacher's lap, according to the Scriptures: "Carry them in thy bosom, as a nursing father carrieth the sucking child"; and "I taught Ephraim to walk, taking them by their arms."

Then a slate is brought, on which the aleph-bet is written, and the teacher should read aloud to the child, "Aleph, bet, gimel, dalet, he, vav," and then in reverse order, "Tav, shin, resh, koph." Then the child is to repeat these letters after the teacher. Thereupon the teacher should read the verse, "Moses commanded us a law, an inheritance of the congregation of Jacob," and then the first sentence from the Third Book of Moses, and the child should speak along with him, word for word. Then a little honey should be put on the slate, and the child should lick the honey from the letters. Thereupon the father should take the child again, and carry it home, and in such a wise that the child may see nothing unclean. And it is right that on this day both father and mother fast and pray to God in heaven that the child may prosper in the Torah and the fear of God, and in good works all his days and his years. But in the evening, when the fast is over, they should prepare a meal for the poor and do charity according to their means. Then verily the father's heart may have firm faith that the fear of God will rest upon this child. These instructions will suffice.

But great will be the merit of those women who are denied children, if the husband rears an orphan in his home and if both strive to guide it along the straight path, as if it were their own child. And if it is within his power to take into his house those who are learning the Torah, and to provide for them, that thus his house may be full of Torah, then, indeed, hail to him and to his destiny! We find the like of this in the case of Rashi,[1] blessed be his memory, who, when he emigrated from France, was a guest in the house of a rich elder. This rich elder besought him to stay in his house and there to study the Torah. And because the rich man besought him, and begged him, Rashi, blessed be his memory, composed a book and named it for the rich elder. In doing this, however, Rashi, blessed be his memory, intended also to exalt and honor others who practice charity. And so, happy the man who selects a fair and pleasant place in his house and destines it for the learning of the Torah. For the Holy One, blessed be he, is present in the house where the Torah is being learned, and the honor of this house will be great in time to come. For when the scattered people of Israel will be gathered, the houses of learning and the houses of prayer will also be gathered in the land of Israel, and will be full of glorious beauty. Amen.

[1] Cf. Index.

THE JOURNEY: A PARABLE FOR
CHILDREN TO BE TOLD ON
THE DAYS OF AWE

Jacob ben Wolf Kranz

Lithuania—Volhynia, 18th Century

FROM OHEL YAAKOB

And to you too, holy children, to you, lovely boys, will I relate a parable that will enable you to know and grasp how greatly it is your duty to strive and to strengthen your souls, so that you may pour out your spirit before our Holy King, blessed be he, on the Days of Awe, the days that are coming toward us in peace.

This is a parable of a father who went on a journey with his little son. And thus was their manner of going: whenever they came to a place that was narrow, or difficult to traverse, such as a river, or a mountain, or a hill, the father lifted his son to his shoulder and strode through that difficult place with him. Once they came to a walled city and the day had ebbed to evening. The gates were shut, and there were only narrow windows in the side of the wall. Then the father said to his son: "You know, my son, that up to now, I have spared you much travail, that I lifted you on my shoulder and took you in my arms. But now—you can see it with your own eyes—there is no way to get into this city, and it is not given into our hands to go through the gate, unless you, my son, strive to climb through the holes and the windows of the wall, and open the gate for me from within."

With this we may compare the following: You know, holy little ones, that we load nothing of the cares, and the duties, and the concerns we must wrestle with, upon our children, and that parents satisfy all the needs of their little ones. But it is not thus today, when we come in prayer and turning to enter the courts of our God, for the gates of prayer are bolted, according to the saying, "When the House of Holiness was destroyed, from that day on the gates of prayer were bolted," [1] and there is no space through which our prayers can enter, unless you see to it, you about whom it is written: "They were swifter than eagles." See! Like birds flying aloft, you have the power to rise, to enter the holy place, and to open the doors of mercy to us, if you pray from the depths of your heart—to widen a crack, to open to us the gates of light, the gates of grace and of mercy. For the pleading of children is the breath of their mouths, and it is a breath without sin. It flings wide the windows of the vaults of heaven and God will hearken to the cry and to the prayer.

THE HONOR DUE TO PARENTS

from the Talmud and the Midrash

"Honor thy father and thy mother, that thy days may be long upon the land which the Lord thy God giveth thee."

"Ye shall fear every man his mother and his father, and ye shall keep My sabbaths: I am the Lord your God."

ON A PAR

Our masters taught:
   It is written, "Honour thy father and thy mother," and it is written, "Honour the Lord with thy substance." The Scriptures put on a par the honoring of father and mother and the honoring of the Omnipresent.

   It is written, "Ye shall fear every man his mother and his father," and it is written, "Thou shalt fear the Lord thy God, and Him shalt thou serve." The Scriptures put on a par the fear of father and mother, and the fear of the Omnipresent.

1 Berakot 32 b.

It is written, "And he that curseth his father, or his mother, shall surely be put to death," and it is written, "Whosoever curseth his God shall bear his sin." The Scriptures put on a par the cursing of father or mother, and the cursing of the Omnipresent.

THE THREE

Our masters taught:
Three participate in a man—the Holy One, blessed be he, and father and mother.
Every time a man honors his father and his mother, the Holy One, blessed be he, says:
"I shall reward them as though I had dwelt among them, and they had honored me."

HONOR AND FEAR

It has been taught: Rabbi Judah the Prince says[1]:
It is open and known to Him who spoke and the world was created,
that the child honors his mother more than his father,
for it is she who sways him by her words;
and so the Holy One, blessed be he, set the honoring of the father before the honoring of the mother.
And it is open and known to Him who spoke and the world was created,
that the child fears his father more than his mother,
for it is he who teaches him the Torah;
and so the Holy One, blessed be he, set the fearing of the mother before the fearing of the father.

HOW FAR?

Rabbi Tarfon had a mother.
Whenever she wished to climb into her bed,
he bowed his body, so that she might climb,
and whenever she wished to come down from her bed,

1 This interpretation is based on the change of sequence in naming father and mother in the verses on honoring and fearing quoted above.

she came down over him.
Then he went and boasted in the house of study.
They said to him:
"Not yet have you accomplished the half of honoring."

THE STEPS

Rabbi Joseph,
when he heard the sound of his mother's steps, said:
"I shall rise before the Divine Presence that is coming."

HONOR DUE TO PARENTS AND TO GOD

Rabbi Simeon ben Yohai said:
Great is the honoring of father and mother;
yes, the Holy One, blessed be he, even gave it precedence
over the honor due to him.
It is written,
"Honor thy father and thy mother,"
and it is written,
"Honor the Lord with thy substance."
Wherewith can you honor him?
With that wherewith he has endowed you:
You set aside the gleaning, the forgotten sheaf at the corner
of the field;
you set aside the heave offering, the first tithe, the second
tithe,
the tithe for the poor, and the loaf;
you see to the booth, and the branch of the palm tree, the
ram's horn, the phylacteries and the fringes [1];
you give food to the poor and the hungry, and you slake
those who thirst.
If you have substance, you are bound to do all of this,
if you have none, you are not bound to do this.
But when it comes to the honoring of father and mother,
it is all the same whether you have something to give, or
have nothing to give:

[1] Offerings and tithes: cf. Lev. 19:19; Num. 15:17–21; Deut. 14:22–29, 24:19. Booth and palm tree branch (for Sukkot): cf. Lev. 23:33–44. Ram's horn: cf. Num. 29:1; Lev. 25:9–17. Phylacteries: tradition based on Deut. 6:8. Fringes: cf. Num. 15:37–41.

"Honor thy father and thy mother"—
even if you have to go begging at doors.

SERVICE

Rabbi Hezekiah said:
It is told about a gentile of Askelon who was chief of the
    councilmen:
On the stone upon which his father sat
he never seated himself;
when his father died,
he idolized the stone.

THE MOTHER

Rabbi Abbahu said:
Rabbi Eliezer the Great was questioned by his disciples:
"What is the honoring of father and mother?"
Said he to them:
"Go and see what Dama, the son of Netina in Askelon,
    has done.
His mother was affected in mind;
she used to strike him when he was with his friends.
He, however, said nothing but,
'It is enough, mother.' "

PRECEDENCE

Our masters taught:
If he, his father, and his teacher are in captivity:
he takes precedence over his teacher,
his teacher takes precedence over his father.
His mother takes precedence over all.

ON THE PRECEPT OF HONORING ONE'S PARENTS

Joseph Karo

Spain—Palestine, 16th Century

FROM THE SHULHAN ARUK

We must be deeply intent upon honoring father and mother, and upon fearing them.

What is fearing? The son must not stand in that place which is his father's when he stands with his friends in a council of elders, nor in that place which is his when he prays, nor may he sit in that place in his house which is his own to lean on, nor contradict his words nor outvote his words in his presence. He must not call him by name, not while he is living and not when he is dead, but say: "My father, my master."

How far does fearing go? If the son is clad in rich raiment and sitting at the head of an assembly, and his father and mother come and tear his garments, strike his head, and spew in his face, he is not to upbraid them for this, but keep silence and fear the King of kings who bade him do this thing.

What is honoring? He shall give his father food and drink, clothe and cover him, lead him in and guide him out, and give to him, and in all this show him a joyful countenance. For though he feed him with fattened meat every day, if he show him an unwilling face, he will be punished for this.

That he should give him food and drink means that he should furnish this from the substance of father and mother—if the father has thereof. But if the father has nothing, and the son has, he is compelled to support his father according to his means. If, however, the son has nothing, he is not in duty bound to go begging at doors in order to feed his father.

But he is in duty bound to honor him with his body, even if he must give up his work for this and beg at doors. But the son need do this only on such days on which he

has the wherewithal to feed himself. If he has it not, he is
not in duty bound to give up his work and go begging at
doors.

If the son needs something from the city, and knows
they will give him what he wishes for his father's sake,
then, even though he knows that they would do it also for
his sake, let him not say, "Do this thing for my sake," but,
"Do it for my father's sake," thus to make the honor he
receives dependent upon his father.

It is his duty to rise before his father, but if the father
is the son's pupil, each rises before the other.

How far does honoring father and mother go? If they
take from him a golden cup and cast it into the sea before
his eyes, he shall not insult them, bring grief upon them,
direct anger against them, but he shall accept the command of the Scriptures, and be silent.

It is the son's duty to honor his father even after his
death. How? If he utters something he has heard from
his lips, he must say: "Thus spoke my father, my master;
may I be the atonement for his resting place," [1] if it is
within the twelve months after his death. But if it is after
the twelve months, he must say: "Blessed be his memory."

If his father or his mother is affected in mind, he must
strive to deal with them according to what they can grasp,
until they find mercy. But should it be impossible to exist
in this way, because their madness is too great, he must
go away and leave them behind, and order others to serve
them as is proper.

If he sees that his father has transgressed the words of
the Torah, he must not say, "You have transgressed the
words of the Torah," but he must say to him, "Father, in
the Torah thus and so it is written," as if he wanted to ask
him about it, not to reproach him, so that in this way he
will understand by himself and not feel ashamed. If the
father has cited some tradition wrongly, the son shall not
say: "Do not teach thus."

If his father say to him, "Give me water," but the son
is faced with the doing of a commandment, the specified

---

1 Kiddushin 31 b; cf. Rashi: "Let all the punishment that his soul
may have to suffer, come upon me."

time for which is passing, such as burying one dead, or accompanying him to the grave, then, if it is possible to have the commandment done by another, the son shall occupy himself with honoring his father. But if none other is at hand to do it, he shall occupy himself with the commandment and omit honoring his father.

Learning the Torah is a greater thing than honoring father and mother.

Should his father tell him to transgress the words of the Torah, whether they be mandatory or prohibitory laws, or even only commandments according to the words of the sages, he shall not obey him.

If a father has forbidden his son to speak with a certain person, or to forgive him before a set time has elapsed, but the son would give up his anger at once, were it not for his father's prohibition, then he shall not heed this prohibition.

A child sprung from incest is in duty bound to honor his father and to fear him; even if his father is a wicked man, one who commits transgressions, the son must honor him and fear him.

A man shall not let his yoke rest heavily upon his children, nor shall he be exacting with them concerning the honor due to him, lest he cause them to stumble. He shall forgive them and hide his eyes from their doing, for: A father who renounces the honor due to him, his renunciation holds.

Whosoever strikes his grown son, him they were wont to banish,[1] for he transgresses in this way: "Thou shalt not put a stumbling block before the blind."

A man must honor his father's wife, even if she is not his mother; this holds as long as his father is alive. And he must honor his mother's husband, as long as his mother is alive. But after her death, he is not bound to honor him. In any case, however, it is an estimable act to honor him even after his mother's death.

[1] A lesser degree of excommunication (*nidduy*), lasting "no less than thirty days."

THE MISSION OF WOMAN

Jonah ben Abraham Gerondi

Spain, 13th Century

FROM THE IGGERET HA-TESHUBAH

"Thus shalt thou say to the house of Jacob, and tell the children of Israel." That hour when the Torah was given to us, Moses, our master, peace be with him, was bidden to speak first to the house of Jacob, and this means to the women.

And why was he bidden to speak first to the women? Because it is they who send their sons to school; because they keep an eye upon their sons, so that these may occupy themselves with the Torah; because they tend them when they come home from school, and move their hearts with good words, so that their longing be directed to the Torah, and they watch over them, lest they go idle instead of learning the Torah; because they teach them the fear of sin, even in childhood, as it is written: "Train up a child in the way he should go, and even when he is old, he will not depart from it."

Thus we find that virtuous women beget love for the Torah and for fearing God. And that is why virtuous women can save the souls of their menfolk. When the men come each from the work he performs, when they are exhausted and weary and do not remember to give some part of their labors and the thoughts of their heart to the Torah, it is the duty of women to remind them to open the book, to busy themselves with the words of the Torah, and not to give their attention to idle matters. For the punishment for idling in regard to the Torah is greater than for transgressing all the commandments in the Torah.

Let them also remind their menfolk to look into this epistle about turning to God that we have composed. Let them make known the words of this epistle both to their menfolk and to their children, and through these words they will become worthy of the life in the coming world.

A woman must see to it that there is peace between herself and her husband; she should be agreeable and kind
to her husband.

A woman must see to it that she prays for her sons and
her daughters, morning and evening, that they learn to
fear heaven, and that her sons prosper in the study of the
Torah and in doing the commandments. For the root of
woman's worthiness in the coming world is that her children fear God's name, and do the will of God, blessed be
he. And when in time she is in her eternal home, and her
children live in the Torah and the fear of heaven, this is
accredited to her as though she were alive, and she is on
the upper steps leading to the coming world.

And when she is intent upon good works, in this hour,
and with pure hands, let her pray that her children become
such as fear heaven, and that they prosper in the Torah
and in doing the commandments. And the reason for this
is that man's prayer is heard at the hour in which he is
doing a commandment. It was the custom of one of the
wise men to give a coin, as a righteous deed, at the hour
in which he went to pray, in order to make real what is
written: "I shall behold Thy face in righteousness."

BUT BY MY SPIRIT

THE TEACHING AND THE TEACHERS

from the Talmud and the Midrash

THE KEEPERS

Rabbi Judah the Prince asked Rabbi Dosa and Rabbi Ammi to go forth and inspect the cities in the Land of Israel.

They came to a city and said to the people: "Have the keepers of the city brought before us."

They brought the overseer and the senator.

Then they said to them: "Are these the keepers of the city? Why, these are the destroyers of the city!"

Then the people asked them: "Who are the keepers of the city?"

Thereupon they answered: "The teachers of the Scriptures and of the Tradition, who keep watch by day and by night, in accordance with the words: 'This book of the law shall not depart out of thy mouth, but thou shalt meditate therein day and night.'"

THE DECISIONS

Rabbi Abba said in the name of Samuel:

For three years the school of Shammai and the school of Hillel were opposed to each other.

The one said: "The law is in accordance with our views!"

The other said: "The law is in accordance with our views!"

Then a voice sped forth from heaven and said:

"Both these words, and those, are the words of the living God, but the law is according to the school of Hillel!"
But if both these words, and those, are the words of the living God, through what has the school of Hillel become worthy of having the law decided according to its interpretation?
Because it was kindly and humble and studied the views held by the school of Shammai along with its own.
And more than this: it set the views of the school of Shammai before its own.

THE TOOL

They questioned Rabban Johanan ben Zakkai:
"A sage who fears sin—what is he?"
He answered them: "He is an artisan with his tools in his hands."
"A sage who does not fear sin—what is he?"
He answered them: "He is an artisan without tools in his hands."
"A man who fears sin, but is not a sage—what is he?"
He answered them: "He is a man who is no artisan, but one who has tools in his hands."

HEREDITY

Why is it that sages do not have sons who are also sages?
Rab Joseph says:
So that no one shall think the Torah can be inherited.
Rab Shisha, the son of Rab Idi, says:
So that they shall not consider themselves superior to the rest of the community.

SCHOLARS AND KINGS

Our masters taught:
A sage takes precedence over a king of Israel;
if a sage dies, we have none like him—
if a king dies, all Israel are eligible for kingship.

WHAT ANIMALS TEACH

Rabbi Johanan said: Had the Torah not been given us, we could have learned modesty from the cat, the command not to rob from the ant, chastity from the dove, and propriety from the cock.

THE DEATH OF RABBI SIMEON BEN LAKISH

The soul of Rabbi Simeon ben Lakish went to its rest, and Rabbi Johanan grieved for him greatly.

Then the masters said: "Who will go to quiet him?"

"Let Rabbi Eleazar ben Pedat go, for his teachings are subtle."

He went and sat down opposite him. To everything Rabbi Johanan said, he replied: "There is a teaching that supports you."

Then the other said: "Are you as the son of Lakish? Whenever I discussed something, the son of Lakish asked me four and twenty questions, and I had to contrive four and twenty answers, and thus the tradition grew of itself. But you say: 'There is a teaching that supports you!' Do you think I am unaware that I have spoken rightly?"

He went on rending his robe, and wept: "Where are you, son of Lakish? Where are you, son of Lakish?" He continued to cry out until his reason forsook him.

Then all the masters prayed to God to have mercy upon him, and his soul went to its rest.

FEEDING THE HUNGRY

In the years of the drought, Rabbi Judah the Prince opened his storehouse. He said: "Let those men come who study the Scriptures, the men of the Mishnah, the men of the Gemara, the men of the Halakah, the men of the Haggadah [1]—but the untaught may not come!"

Then Rabbi Jonathan ben Amram pressed forward, entered, and said to him: "Master, feed me!"

He asked him: "My son, have you read the Scriptures?"

The other answered: "No."

[1] Cf. Index, under Talmud.

"Have you learned the Mishnah?"
The other answered: "No."
He asked him: "How then can I feed you?"
The other said to him: "Feed me like a dog, feed me like a crow."
He gave him food. When he had gone away, Rabbi Judah grieved, and said: "Woe is me, that I have given my bread to one who is untaught."
Then Rabbi Simeon, son of Rabbi Judah, said to him: "Perhaps it was your pupil Jonathan ben Amram, who all his life did not wish to profit from the honor given to the Torah?"
They looked into this and found it was true. Then Rabbi Judah said: "Let everyone come."

THE TASK

Rabbi Tarfon used to say:
It is not incumbent upon you to complete the work,
but neither are you free to withdraw from it.

THE COMMANDMENTS ARE ONE

Interpretation of Rabbi Simlai

Babylonia—Palestine, 3d Century

FROM THE TALMUD

Rabbi Simlai expounded thus:
Six hundred and thirteen commandments were given to Moses—three hundred and fifty-six prohibitory laws, equaling the number of days of the solar year, and two hundred and forty-eight mandatory laws, corresponding to the limbs of man.
David came and comprised them in eleven. As it is written:
"Lord, who shall sojourn in Thy tabernacle? Who shall dwell upon thy holy mountain?

He that walketh uprightly, and worketh righteousness, and speaketh the truth in his heart;
That hath no slander upon his tongue, nor doeth evil to his fellow, nor taketh up a reproach against his neighbor. In whose eyes a vile person is despised; but he honoreth them that fear the Lord. He that sweareth to his own hurt, and changeth not.
He that putteth not out his money on interest, nor taketh a bribe against the innocent. He that doeth these things shall never be moved."
Isaiah came and comprised them in six. As it is written:
"He that walketh righteously, and speaketh uprightly; he that despiseth the gain of oppressions, that shaketh his hands from holding of bribes, that stoppeth his ears from hearing of blood, and shutteth his eyes from looking upon evil."
Micah came and comprised them in three. For it is written:
"It hath been told thee, O man, what is good, and what the Lord doth require of thee: Only to do justly, and to love mercy, and to walk humbly with thy God."
And again it was Isaiah who comprised them in two. As it is written:
"Thus saith the Lord: Keep ye justice, and do righteousness."
And Amos came and comprised them in one, as it is said:
"For thus saith the Lord unto the house of Israel: Seek ye Me, and live."
To this Rab Nahman bar Isaac objected and said: That would mean, "Seek me" in observing the entire Torah "and live"! But it is Habakkuk who came and comprised them in one. As it is written: "But the righteous shall live by his faith."

LAW AND JUSTICE

from the Talmud

Once some porters broke a barrel of wine belonging to
Rabbah bar Bar Hanan; so he took their clothing from
them.[1] Thereupon they went to Rab, and he said to
Rabbah: "Give them back their clothing."
Rabbah replied: "Is this the law?"
Rab answered him: "Certainly! It is written: 'That thou
mayest walk in the way of good men.' "
So he gave them back their clothing.
Hereupon they said to Rab: "We are poor and have
toiled all through the day; now we are hungry and we
have nothing."
Then Rab said to Rabbah: "Go and pay them their
wages."
Rabbah replied: "Is this the law?"
Rab answered him: "Certainly! It is written: 'And keep
the paths of the righteous.' "

NOT IN HEAVEN

from the Talmud

We learned:
If a stove is taken apart and sand strewed between the
sections, Rabbi Eliezer declares it is clean, the sages that
it is unclean.
It has been taught:
On that day Rabbi Eliezer brought all the proof in the
world, but they did not accept it from him.
Then he said to them: "If the law agrees with me, this
locust tree shall prove it!"
The locust tree was flung a hundred ells out of the soil
where it was rooted; others say four hundred ells.

[1] According to the letter of the talmudic law, the negligent worker is
responsible for the loss.

They said to him: "No proof can be brought from the locust tree."

Then he spoke to them again: "If the law agrees with me, this stream of water shall prove it."

The stream began to flow backward.

They said to him: "No proof can be brought from a stream."

Then he spoke to them again: "If the law agrees with me, the walls of the house of study shall prove it."

The walls of the house of study leaned over, as though they were about to fall.

Then Rabbi Joshua cried out upon them, saying: "Is it any concern of yours if learned men argue with one another about the law?"

So they did not fall, for the sake of Rabbi Joshua's honor, and they did not straighten, for the sake of Rabbi Eliezer's honor, and to this day they stand leaning over.

Then he spoke to them again: "If the law agrees with me, heaven itself shall prove it!"

A voice sped forth from heaven, saying: "Why do you dispute with Rabbi Eliezer—the law agrees with him in every case!"

Then Rabbi Joshua arose and said: " 'It is not in heaven.' "

What did he mean by "not in heaven"? Rabbi Jeremiah says: The Torah was given on Mount Sinai; the voice from heaven does not concern us. For it was written in the Torah on Mount Sinai: "After the majority must one incline."

THE ALLEGORY OF THE LOVER

from the Zohar

Spain, 13th Century

. . . When "the ancient one" had reached this point he paused, and the two rabbis prostrated themselves before him, wept, and said: "Had we come into this world only in order to hear these your words from your mouth, it were sufficient."

Said he: "Colleagues, I did not begin to speak to you merely in order to tell you what I have told up to now, for surely an old man like myself would not limit himself to one saying, making a noise like a single coin in a jug. How many human beings live in confusion of mind, beholding not the way of truth, whose dwelling is in the Torah, the Torah that calls them day by day to herself in love, but alas, they do not even turn their heads! It is indeed as I have said, that the Torah lets out a word and emerges for a little from her sheath, and then hides herself again. But she does this only for those who understand and obey her.

"She is like unto a beautiful and stately maiden who is hidden in a secluded chamber of a palace and has a lover of whom no one knows but she. For love of her he constantly passes by her gate, turning his eyes to all sides to find her. She knows that he is always haunting the palace, and what does she do? She opens a little door in her hidden chamber, for a moment discloses her face to her lover, then swiftly hides it again. None but he notices it; but his heart, and his soul, and all that is in him are drawn to her, knowing as he does that she has revealed herself to him for a moment because she loves him.

"It is the same with the Torah, which reveals her hidden secrets only to those who love her. She knows that he who is wise of heart daily haunts the gates of her house. What does she do? She shows her face to him from her palace, making a sign of love to him, and straightway returns to her hiding place again. No one understands her message save he alone, and he is drawn to her with his heart and soul and all his being. Thus the Torah reveals herself for a moment in love to her lovers, in order to awaken fresh love in them.

"Now this is the way of Torah. At the first, when she begins to reveal herself to a man, she makes signs to him. If he understands, well and good, but if not, she sends for him and calls him 'simpleton.' When he comes to her she begins to speak to him, first from behind the curtain that she has spread before her words so that they may be suitable to his mode of understanding, so that he may progress little by little. This is called derasha.[1] Then she speaks to him from behind a thin veil of a finer mesh, speaking in riddles and parables, which go by the name of haggadah.[2] When at last he is familiar with her, she shows herself to him face to face and converses with him concerning all her hidden mysteries and all the mysterious ways that have been secreted in her heart from time immemorial. Then such a man is a true adept in the Torah, a 'master of the house,' since she has revealed to him all her mysteries, withholding and hiding nothing. She says to him: 'Do you see the sign, the hint, that I gave you at first, how many mysteries it contains?' He realizes then that nothing may be added to nor taken from the words of the Torah, not even one sign or letter. Therefore men should follow the Torah with might and main in order that they may become her lovers as has been described."

ON BOOKS AND ON WRITING

Judah ibn Tibbon

Spain, 12th Century

FROM HIS TESTAMENT [3]

I have honored you by providing an extensive library for your use, and have thus relieved you of the necessity of borrowing books. Most students must bustle about to seek books, often without finding them. But you, thanks be to God, lend and borrow not. Of many books, indeed, you own two or three copies. I have besides made for you books

1 Talmudic casuistry, i.e., derivation of the traditional laws and usages from the letter of the Scripture.
2 Symbolic interpretation.
3 Addressed to his son, Samuel ibn Tibbon, a physicist and philosopher, who translated the Moreh Nebukim of Maimonides from Arabic into Hebrew.

on all sciences,[1] hoping that your hand may "find all as a nest."

My son! Make your books your companions, let your cases and shelves be your pleasure grounds and gardens. Bask in their paradise, gather their fruit, pluck their roses, take their spices and their myrrh. If your soul be satiate and weary, change from garden to garden, from furrow to furrow, from prospect to prospect. Then will your desire renew itself and your soul be filled with delight!

My son! Take it upon yourself to write one leaf daily and to meditate for an hour in the *Ben Mishle*.[2] Read every week the pentateuchal section in Arabic. This will improve your Arabic vocabulary, and will be of advantage in translating, if you should feel inclined to translate.

My son! If you write, read it through a second time, for no man can avoid slips. Let not any consideration of hurry prevent you from revising a short epistle. Be punctilious as to grammatical accuracy, in conjugation and genders, for the constant use of the vernacular sometimes leads to error in this regard. A man's mistakes in writing bring him into disrepute; they are remembered against him all his days. As our sages say: "Who is it that uncovers his nakedness here, and it is exposed everywhere? It is he who writes a document and makes mistakes therein." Be careful in the use of conjunctions and adverbs [particles], and how you apply them and how they harmonize with the verbs. I have already begun to compose for you a book on this subject, to be called "Principles of Style," may God permit me to complete it! And whatever you are in doubt about and have no book to aid in, abstain from expressing it! Endeavor to cultivate conciseness and elegance, do not attempt to write verse unless you can do it perfectly. Avoid heaviness, which spoils a composition, making it disagreeable alike to reader and audience.

1 Apparently referring to compendia made for the son's use.
2 Ben Mishle ("Son of Proverbs") is a series of metrical aphorisms based on the biblical Books of Proverbs (Mishle); its author is Samuel ha-Nagid, a statesman and scholar of Granada contemporary with the writer.

See to it that your handwriting is as beautiful as your style. Keep your pen in fine working order, use ink of good color. Make your script as perfect as possible, unless you are forced to write without proper materials, or in a pressing emergency. The beauty of a composition depends on the writing, and the beauty of the writing on pen, paper, and ink; and all these excellences are an index of the author's worth.

Examine your Hebrew books at every new moon, the Arabic volumes once in two months, and the bound copies once every quarter. Arrange your library in fair order, so as to avoid wearying yourself in searching for the book you need. Always know the case and chest where the book should be. A good plan would be to place in each compartment a written list of the books therein contained. If, then, you are looking for a book, you can see from the list the exact shelf it occupies, without disarranging all the books in the search for one. Examine the loose leaves in the volumes and bundles, and preserve them. These sheets contain very important matters that I collected and copied out. Do not destroy any writing or letter of all that I have left. And cast your eye frequently over the catalogue, in order to remember what books are in your library.

Never refuse to lend books to anyone who has not the means to purchase books for himself, but only lend to those who can be trusted to return the volumes. You know what our sages said in the Talmud on the text, "Wealth and riches are in his house; and his merit endureth for ever." [1] But "withhold not good from him to whom it is due," and take particular care of your books. Cover the bookcases with rugs of fine quality; and preserve them from damp and mice, and from all manner of injury, for your books are your greatest treasure. If you lend a volume, make a memorandum before it leaves your house, and when it is returned strike out the entry with your pen. At each Passover and Tabernacles, call in all books out on loan.

[1] The Talmud (Ketubot 50 a) applies the verse to one who transcribes the Scriptures and lends his copies to others.

Make it a fixed rule in your home to read the Scriptures, and to peruse grammatical works on Sabbaths and festivals, also to read Proverbs and the *Son of Proverbs*.[1] Also, I beg you, look at the chapter concerning Jonadab, son of Rechab, every Sabbath, to instill in you diligence to fulfill my commands.

A COLLECTOR OF BOOKS

Joseph Solomon del Medigo

Crete—Bohemia, 17th Century

FROM HIS LETTER TO THE KARAITE, ZERAH BEN NATHAN

. . . Now do not believe that I have not read those writings which I have failed to mention, for there are not even many non-Jewish writings I have not read—let alone Jewish! But I have selected those which will be of most use to you, so that you will not simply read everything pell-mell and without judgment. I know very well, my son, that there is no book whatsoever that is not potentially of some use to the reader, especially if he has perspicacity and a critical sense. But time is precious. Incidentally, if you want to see beautiful manuscripts, you must go to Constantinople, a city that leads all others in scholarship. Although many treasures there have been destroyed by fire, learned men have spent great effort in saving and copying much. . . .

If you take my advice, you will read the works I have listed, and then you will find that they suffice for everything you need to know. For it is not the quantity of what we read that counts, but its quality. Too much promiscuous reading may even harm beginners, just as too much food hurts children and invalids, and variety of presentation does not serve to increase the stores of the intellect. If merely a great number of books were the road to scholar-

[1] Cf. note 3 above.

ship, the merchants who heap them up in towering piles
would be the true sages. It is not enough to possess books;
one must ponder their contents.

Whoever is fortunate enough to have money, should
fill his house with books, for it is better to have these than
vain baubles, and they delight those who are sad or sated
with life. Even in my earliest youth, I was irresistibly
drawn to books and scarcely slept for eagerness to read
and study. Thank God, I had ample means, did not hesitate to spend money, used many thousands, and bought
as many valuable books as possible with these. Since such
books are widely scattered, I have had them brought from
many different countries, and now my library contains over
seven thousand selected volumes, not counting the instruments skillfully perfected by various artists. Aside from
this collection, I spent much money for such matters on
my journeys.

I owe great thanks to my teacher and father, and to my
mother, who had me instructed in Greek when I was very
young, and so gave me the opportunity to pursue fruitful
studies, since all the writings of the ancient philosophers,
physicians, and astronomers are in Greek. Then I also
learned Latin, Italian, and Spanish, into which old and
new works have been translated. I was even going to learn
Arabic, but I gave up this idea because I realized that
everything beautiful written in this language is taken from
the Greek, with only few and slight changes. And so I have
always gone in quest of knowledge. And now that I have
been driven from my good father's house, now that for
seven years I have had no permanent abode and have been
haunted and bowed by sorrows, I am still faithful to
knowledge. To me, carrying the pen was like girding my
loins, and no matter where I was, I would at night, when
others slept, write down my thoughts, after carefully reflecting on my experiences. From the age of eighteen I
have been in the habit of noting all such things so that
I may not forget them.

GOOD AND BAD BOOKS

Joseph Solomon del Medigo

Crete—Bohemia, 17th Century

FROM NOBLOT HOKMAH

People say that the art of printing has brought us great advantages, whereas it has in fact been detrimental to us. For in former days authors were handsomely paid and people would buy from them only the good, pleasing, useful books, while the useless, vain books would of themselves disappear. Not so, however, in our days, when many ignorant people assume airs, and, though benighted and smaller than the least throughout their lives, seek to set themselves up as shining lights to another generation that has not learned to know them. And everyone who possibly can, and whose wealth is greater than his understanding, connives to publish books in which he is arbitrarily referred to as a great and worthy man, whereas he is no more an authority than is a carpenter's apprentice.

The only concern of publishers is for new books. No one pays any attention to the writings of the early authors, or makes effort to preserve them and to shake the dust from them. Because of the art of printing you find a topsy-turvy world—the native below and the stranger on top.

It seems to me that books are subject to the same process as souls: they migrate from one body to another. Not by chance are son and book designated in Latin by the same term, *liber*. And so it is in the case of scholarly books that are translated from one language into another, in a different style, in other words, and in changed order. The language becomes different but the content is the same. And the book is given a new title—for example, a book originally entitled *Precious Vessel* will be called *Costly Vessel*. The matter remains exactly the same except that it has been poured from one receptacle into another. Ecclesiastes has taught us all this in these his words: "That which hath been is that which shall be, and that which hath been done is that which shall be done; and there is nothing new under the sun. Is there a thing whereof it is said: 'See, this is new'?—it hath been already, in the ages which were before us. There is no remembrance of them of former times; neither shall there be any remembrance of them of latter times that are to come, among those that shall come after." He also said: "Seeing that in the days to come all will long ago have been forgotten."

It is true indeed that there is no cause for concern about the good, useful, pleasing authors, for under any circumstances their names will live for many days, perhaps they will even shine forever, like stars. But not so in the case of those who pen spurious writings, who have consumed their time and their money to no advantage. When their ignorance is laid bare and their mischief gives offense, their shortcomings are recognized and their hope turns to despair. For their eye is dimmed. Even if they were to offer their books as gifts, no one would accept them. They become like thorns in their eyes, they are piled high in their houses, heaps upon heaps, and the rats feed upon and glut themselves with them. And the rain falls, drips down upon them drop upon drop, and the birds, pigeons, and chickens nest among them. The sun sets at noon for the authors of these books, before their very eyes, and their books die in their lifetime.

But if the authors were only wise enough to realize all this, they would recoil from "much study that is a weariness of the flesh." But their love for themselves is great, and they shut their minds to the fact that the ultimate end of their books is but a vain one, for no one would ever commit the folly of publishing them anew. Thus one who writes a number of inferior books will live unto all generations just as little as the name of one who begets many illegitimate children.

IN FAREWELL

from the Talmud

When the masters departed from the house of Rabbi Ammi
　　—some say from the house of Rabbi Hanina—they said to
　　him:
"May you see your world in your life,
may your aim be fulfilled in the life of the coming world,
your hope throughout the generations.
Let your heart meditate in understanding,
your mouth utter wisdom,
your tongue move in songs of jubilation.
May your eyelids set your glance straight before you,[1]
your eyes glow with the light of the Torah,
your face shine with the radiance of heaven,
your lips proclaim knowledge,
your reins rejoice in uprightness,
your feet hasten to hear the words of the Ancient of Days."[2]

[1] In understanding of the Torah.
[2] Cf. Dan. 7:9.

MERCY AND TRUTH

FROM MAN TO MAN

Nahman of Bratzlav

Ukraine, 18th–19th Century

There are men who suffer terrible distress and are unable
to tell what they feel in their hearts, and they go their way
and suffer and suffer. But if they meet one with a laughing
face, he can revive them with his joy. And to revive a man
is no slight thing.

MERCY UPON LIVING CREATURES

from the Talmud and the Midrash

THE SUFFERINGS OF RABBI JUDAH THE PRINCE

The sufferings of Rabbi Judah the Prince, these came upon
him with a certain event, and after a certain other event
they went from him.

They came upon him with a certain event—how was
that? A calf that was being led off to slaughter came and

hid its head in the lap of Rabbi Judah's robe and wept. But he said: "Go, that is what you were created for." Then it was said: "Because he did not have mercy, suffering shall come upon him."

After a certain other event they went from him: One day Rabbi Judah's serving maid was sweeping the house, and she wanted to sweep out and cast forth some young weasels. But he said: "Let them be; it is written: 'The Lord is good to all; and His tender mercies are over all His works.' "

Then it was said: "Because he has shown mercy, mercy shall also be shown to him."

THE SHEPHERDS

"The Lord trieth the righteous." And wherewith does he try him? By having him pasture sheep.

Thus did he try David with sheep, and find him a good shepherd; for he held the bigger sheep back behind the smaller ones, and led the smaller ones first to pasture so that they might graze on the tender tips of grass. Then he led the old sheep there, that they might eat the ordinary blades, and last he led the young sheep there, so that they might feed on the tougher stalks.

Then the Holy One, blessed be he, said: "He who knows how to pasture sheep, each according to its strength, shall come to pasture my people." That is what has been written: "From following the ewes that give suck He brought him, to be shepherd over Jacob His people."

And the Holy One, blessed be he, tried Moses also and in no other wise than with sheep. Our masters said that once when Moses, our master, peace be with him, was pasturing the flock of Jethro, near the desert, a little ram ran away. So he ran after it until it came to a rocky ledge. And when it had reached the rocky ledge, there was a pond, and it stopped to drink. When Moses came up to it, he said: "Why, I did not know that you had run away because you were thirsty. Now you are tired." So he let it ride upon his shoulder and went.

Then the Holy One, blessed be he, said: "You show compassion in thus leading the flock of him who is of flesh and blood. By your life! It is you who shall pasture my flock, Israel."

THE CREATION OF THE WORLD

"In the beginning God created." [1]
It is not written, "The Lord created":
first there rose within his mind the plan
of creating the world with the attribute of justice;
then he saw that thus the world could not endure,
and he set first the attribute of mercy and added it to the
    attribute of justice.
That is why [later] it is written:
"In the day that the Lord God made earth and heaven."

THE IMITATION OF GOD

Rabbi Hama ben Rabbi Hanina said:
It is written: "After the Lord your God shall ye walk."
What does this mean? Is it possible for man to walk after
the Presence of God? Is it not written, "For the Lord thy
God is a devouring fire"? What it means is that we shall
walk after the attributes of the Holy One, blessed be he.

As he clothes the naked—for it is written, "And the Lord
God made for Adam and for his wife garments of skins,
and clothed them"—thus you also shall do: you shall clothe
the naked.

The Holy One, blessed be he, visited the sick, as it is
written: "And the Lord appeared unto him by the tere-
binths of Mamre." Thus you also shall do: you shall visit
the sick.

The Holy One, blessed be he, comforted those who
mourned, as it is written: "And it came to pass after the
death of Abraham, that God blessed Isaac his son." Do
likewise: comfort those who mourn.

The Holy One, blessed be he, buried the dead, as it is
written: "And he was buried in the valley in the land of
Moab." Do likewise; bury the dead.

---

[1] According to Talmudic tradition, the word God is interpreted to
mean "attribute of justice," and Lord is held to signify "attribute of
mercy."

Rabbi Simlai expounded:
The Torah: It begins with the showing of mercy and it
ends with the showing of mercy.

It begins with the showing of mercy, as it is written:
"And the Lord God made for Adam and for his wife garments of skins, and clothed them."

It ends with the showing of mercy, as it is written: "And
he was buried in the valley in the Land of Moab."

THE LOVE OF ONE'S NEIGHBOR AND
THE LOVE OF GOD

Samuel Laniado

Syria, 16th Century

FROM KLI HEMDAH

It is true that among the duties to be observed there is also
this—to love one's neighbor as one's own life, and this quite
literally, as it is written, "Love for your neighbor as for
yourself,"[1] really "as for yourself," but since this is very
remote to one, because nothing is more important to a
person than his own being, and nothing dearer to him
than himself, the Scriptures took this into consideration,
and it is written "for your neighbor"; but it is not written
to love your neighbor as yourself, for this, as we have said,
would be impossible. It is, however, man's duty—and in
doing it, the community can well endure—to love those
things that pertain to his neighbor, whether it be his business, or his honor. Love for your neighbor what is useful,
and right, and good, just as you do for yourself. And this
means that just as a man who has hurt himself with his
hand, will not avenge or bear a grudge, and hurt in return
the hand that has hurt him, so it is if a neighbor inflicts
pain or the like upon him: he will not avenge, or bear a

1 This translation indicates Laniado's interpretation of the verse. The
usual translation is: "Thou shalt love thy neighbor as thyself."

grudge, because he regards this neighbor as himself, as his very self. And that is why the commandment reads: "Thou shalt not take vengeance, nor bear any grudge against the children of thy people."

That is why it is written: "Thou shalt not take vengeance, nor bear any grudge against the children of thy people," and "Love for your neighbor as for yourself." This indicates that the two things are related to each other. "Thou shalt not take vengeance, nor bear any grudge" follows from "love for your neighbor."

Furthermore it is said: "I am the Lord," and this explains two things. First, since the souls that are as they should be, are all a part of God, and since the soul of one man and the soul of his neighbor are both carved out of the same throne of Splendor, therefore "love for your neighbor as for yourself" is meant literally, for he is as you. Since I, God, am he who created your soul and the soul of your neighbor, he is as you. And, second, if your love for your neighbor is as the love for yourself, this is considered love for me, because "I am the Lord." Since your love for him is like the love for yourself, even for him who is an infinitesimal part of me—how much more will you love me! For the love for your neighbor will be considered as if I, God, had myself received it.

And so in Israel we find those three characteristics— mercy, a sense of shame, and charity; [1] for although they are separate in body, they are all one in soul, because each regards the other as a part of God, as it is written: "I said: Ye are godlike beings, and all of you sons of the Most High."

[1] Yebamot 79 a.

THE UGLY IMPLEMENT

from Derek Erez Rabbah

2d–3d Century

This is a story about Rabbi Simeon ben Eleazar, who was returning from Migdal-Eder, from the house of his master. He rode on a donkey, ambling along the seashore in a leisurely fashion. There he came upon a man who was exceedingly ugly to look upon. He said to him: "Amazing how ugly the children of our father Abraham can be!"

Said the other to him: "What shall I do? Tell it to the artist who made me."

Immediately Rabbi Simeon ben Eleazar got down from his donkey, prostrated himself before the other, and said: "I bow down to you; forgive me!"

Said the other to him: "I cannot forgive you until you go to the artist who made me, and say to him: 'How ugly is this implement you have made!'"

But the rabbi walked after him for half a mile. Then the people of his town heard of it, went forth to meet him, and said to him: "Peace be with you, master!"

Said the ugly one to them: "Whom do you address as master?"

Said they to him: "Him who is walking behind you."

Said he to them: "If that is a master, may there not be many like him in Israel!"

Said they to him: "God forfend! What has he done to you?"

And he told them the whole matter. And they urged him greatly to forgive. He said: "Very well, I forgive him, provided he does not make a habit of saying such things."

On this day Rabbi Simeon sat in his great house of study, taught and expounded: Always be supple as the reed, not rigid as a cedar. A reed, even though the four winds of the world ride forth, the reed bends with them and straightens with them; when the winds are still, the reed again stands in its place. And the end of this reed? It is considered worthy for the making of the pen that writes the scroll of the Torah. But not so with the cedar: if a wind blows from the northwest, it tears it down; if it blows from the south-west, it blows it down and hurls it upon its face. And thus it is found: cast down is the cedar that stood so high upon its roots. And the end of this cedar? Loggers come and chop it up and use it to build houses, and what is left they throw into the fire.

This is why the sages said: Be supple as a reed; do not be rigid as a cedar.

THE TRUE PHYSICIAN

Asaph Judaeus

Mesopotamia, 7th Century

ADMONITION TO HIS PUPILS

The master speaks:

Beware of causing death to anyone by administering the juices of poisonous roots. Do not administer to an adulterous wife an abortifacient drug. Let not the beauty of women arouse in you the desire for adultery. Divulge not any secret entrusted to you and do no act of injury or of harm for any price. Do not close your heart to mercy toward the poor and the needy. Say not of good that it is evil, nor of evil that it is good. Walk not in the path of sorcerers who raise enmity in married couples through incantation, magic, and witchcraft. Do not covet any possession as a reward for having aided in an act of infamy. In your treatment, do not apply the arts of the idolater, and place no trust in idols, for they are naught and of no avail. Put your trust in the Lord, the God of truth; he kills and he brings to life; he punishes and he heals the wound; he gives to man understanding for being of help; he punishes in righteousness and justice, but he re-stores in love and in mercy; he causes healing herbs to grow and he implants into the perfect heart the ability to heal, in order to make known his great grace and his won-

drous works before great multitudes, so that all who live
may understand that he is the Creator and that besides
him there is none who can help. The nations place their
trust in idols that cannot help them in the hour of need,
nor save them in their distress; thus their hope and their
longings lead to death. It is proper, therefore, that you
separate yourselves from them, that you keep yourselves
far removed from their idols, and that you call upon the
name of the Lord, the living God, the God of the spirits
of all flesh, in whose hand lies power over the souls of all
the living and the spirits of all mankind, to kill or to bring
to life; no one can escape his might. Keep him in mind at
all times, seek him in truth, rectitude, and perfection; then
will all the works of your hands succeed. He will help you
to be of aid to others and all mankind will give you praise;
the people will foresake their idols for the service of the
Lord, for they will recognize that they have placed their
trust in naught, that they have wearied themselves in vain
in the service of gods that are of no avail.

Therefore be you strong and not indolent, for great
reward awaits your work. God will be with you, if you are
with him. If you keep the covenant of your oath and if
you follow our instructions, then you will be honored as
saints in the eyes of all mankind, who will say: "Happy
is the nation whose God is the Lord; the people whom He
hath chosen for His own inheritance."

The pupils answer:
Everything concerning which you have admonished us,
and everything which you have enjoined upon us, we shall
heed, for it is the law of the Torah, and it is our duty to
obey it with pure heart, with whole soul, and with all our
strength, and not to depart from it either to the right or
to the left.

The master:
See the Lord, his holiness and his Torah are witnesses
that you fear him and that you will not swerve from his
laws, but that you will follow his commandments and that
you will not depart from the straight path in order to gain
profit from helping him who is lying in wait for the inno-

cent soul or from him who mixes poison to kill. Do not
make known to anyone which plants are poisonous, nor
give them to anyone. Allow no one to persuade you in any
manner to produce disease in anyone. Take heed lest you
cause any bodily deformity whatsoever and be not too
much in haste to apply the knife. Do not apply cupping
immediately. Only when you have considered and examined carefully two and three times, only then may you
apply this remedy. Beware lest the spirit of pride come
upon you and lest you bear vengeful hate against any sick
one. In your speech be upright and truthful, then will you
find grace in the eyes of God, and among men be regarded
as honest, trustworthy, and upright physicians.

THE DISEASED WIFE

Solomon ben Isaac (Rashi)

France—Germany, 11th Century

A RESPONSUM

Reuben and Simeon [1] brought their suit before Rabbi Solomon:

Reuben's wife was bringing complaint against him because he had driven her from his house and was not treat-
ing her according to Jewish law, whereas he claimed: "I
have driven you out according to law so that you cannot
bind me to the marriage contract.[2] For I made a false bargain in you. It is obvious that you are stricken with leprosy
and that you show signs of leprosy in that boils are spread
all over your nose and over your face in general. Also, you
noticed this malady in you even before our marriage.

1 These names are used in legal literature as examples.
2 The marriage contract (ketubah) provides for a money payment to
the woman in the event of the husband's death or of a divorce when
she is guiltless. The woman loses her right to this settlement if she
has a bodily defect that was unknown to the husband before marriage.

There are some members of your family who have suffered from this ailment and at the time I married you I did not detect the latent blemishes in you." She, however, said: "It is not so. I entered upon our marriage in perfect health. As for your saying that I show symptoms of leprosy, that was and is altogether impossible. For my whole body is perfect except for two moles that grew on my face out of sorrow and aggravation after you drove me from your house."

And some members of the community testified to that, saying that they had dwelt with him for several years and had never heard him speak of this. For she entered upon marriage in full health and they detected no symptoms of leprosy in her.

To these contending statements the rabbi gave the following reply:

I greet the signers of this inquiry. In view of the fact that no blemish was detected in the woman while she was in her father's house, and since the blemishes appeared after she came under her husband's authority, the latter has no claim against her on the ground of any blemishes. The husband has displayed evil conduct and has shown that he is not of the seed of Abraham our father, who was wont to show mercy toward all creatures and especially toward his own kind with whom he had entered into a covenant. If he had set his heart upon drawing her near to him as he has set his heart upon rejecting her, he would have found her attractive. For thus have our sages said: "Every place has an attraction for its inhabitants" [1]:—even though that place be polluted by infested waters and its soil wreak ruin; likewise is "the attraction of a wife for her husband," and happy is he who has acquired merit through her and gained life in the coming world through her. For even among those who disbelieve in the Holy One, blessed be he, we see many who do not reject their wives, having in mind that "the good deeds of the nations serve as a sin offering," [2] and so the wives also act in the same way toward their husbands. But this one has hardened himself against the very house of our Father in heaven. . . .

The judgment and verdict against him are that he treat

1 Sotah 47 a.
2 Talmudic interpretation of Prov. 14:34.

her as is due the daughters of Israel, and if he does not
reinstate her with mercy and with honor, let him divorce
her and give her all that is stipulated in her marriage
contract.

THE SERVANT

Moses Maimonides

Spain—Egypt, 12th Century

FROM THE MISHNEH TORAH

The law permits that a Canaanite slave be subjected to
hard labor. Nevertheless, though that is the law, the quality
of kindness and the way of wisdom demand that man
should show mercy and pursue justice and never weigh
down the yoke of his servant, nor do him harm. One
should give him unreservedly of every food and of every
drink. The early sages used to serve their servants every
dish they themselves ate and let their cattle and their
servants eat even before they themselves ate. As, behold,
the Psalmist has said: "As the eyes of servants unto the
hand of their master, as the eyes of a maiden unto the
hand of her mistress." Similarly shall he not abuse his
servant, by either an unkind deed or an unkind word.
The Torah has consigned the Canaanites to slavery, not
to shame. Nor shall he heap loud reproach or pile anger
upon him; he shall speak to him softly and listen to his
pleas. And so it is clearly brought out in the case of Job's
noble ways, in which he took pride: "If I did despise the
cause of my manservant or of my maidservant, when they
contended with me, what then shall I do when God riseth
up? And when he remembereth, what shall I answer Him?
Did not He that made me in the womb make him? And
did not One fashion us in the womb?"

Cruelty and highhandedness are to be found only among
idolatrous pagans. But the seed of Abraham, our father,
that is, Israel, upon whom the Holy One, blessed be he,

showered the blessing of the Torah, appointing unto them righteous laws and judgments, should be merciful unto all. Thus, with reference to the qualities of the Holy One, blessed be he, which we were commanded to emulate, the psalmist says: "And His tender mercies are over all His works." And all those who show mercy will have mercy shown unto them, as it is said: "And He shall pour mercy upon thee and shall have compassion upon thee and multiply thee."

A STORY OF THE RICH MAN AND THE BEGGAR

from the Maasiyot

The sages told:

There was a man, a very, very rich man. But in his heart he thought: "What profit have I of all my labor? What will my riches and my fortune avail me in the hour of my death?" Then people told him to be charitable, to do good with his fortune, and that this would accompany him in his world and be provision for his journey. For riches do not endure and are apt to vanish swiftly, as it is written: "Wilt thou set thine eyes upon it? It is gone." Then he swore to do good with his fortune only to a man who had despaired and lost faith in this world.

One day it came to pass: When he went forth, beyond the precincts of his city, he found a poor man who was sitting in filth and had covered himself with all manner of torn rags. Then he spoke in his heart: "Verily, this man has despaired of goodness in this world, and is awaiting death, for he is in great trouble and can have no faith in this world." So he gave him a hundred dinars. But the poor man was astonished and said to him: "Why do you give this money to me alone? Why do you not divide it among all the poor in the city?"

Said he to him: "Because I have sworn to practice charity

only toward one who has despaired of goodness in this world."

Then the needy man said to him: "Take back your money, fool and dolt that you are! You yourself have despaired of goodness in this world, but I trust in the compassion of God and await his mercy at every moment and at all times, as it is written: 'The Lord is good to all; and His tender mercies are over all His works.' Have you not read: 'He raiseth up the poor out of the dust, He lifteth up the needy from the dung-hill'? Do you not know that there is nothing to keep him from making me rich and saving me from these tribulations? Give up this foolishness, put it from you, and all will be well with you."

Said the rich man to him: "Do you reward my mercy by mocking me and spurning me?"

Said the poor man to him: "You thought to have done good to me, but this is not so; rather have you killed me, for no one despairs of goodness in the world save the dead."

Then the rich man spoke in his heart: "If this be so, I shall go and bury this fortune of mine in the graveyard with the dead, who despair of the goodness of the world." And he did so.

Time passed. The rich man grew needy, and had nothing left. When he saw that life had become so straitened, he went and dug in the graveyard to bring up his buried treasure and support himself therewith. Then the watchmen found him, seized him, and brought him before the elder of the city.

But the poor man who had sat in filth, had been appointed elder of the city, because he was the child of a good family, and so, when the elder of the city died, the people of the precinct had gathered and made the poor man their ruler and commander. Then it came to pass: When they brought before him the man who had been digging in the graveyard, they said to him: "Sir, we found this man digging among the graves, to rob the dead of their shrouds."

Then the elder looked upon him and knew him, but made himself strange unto him, and spoke to him, saying: "What deed is this that you have done? As truly as my soul lives, you deserve to die."

Said the other to him: "My lord, God forfend! It never came into my mind to do such a disgraceful thing, but thus and thus it was with me"—and then he told him all that had happened concerning that which he had hidden in the graveyard.

Then the elder said to him: "Do you not recognize me?" The other said: "How should a servant recognize his lord?"

Said the elder to him: "I am that poor man who sat in filth, and you said to yourself that I had despaired of goodness in the world." He rose, went toward him, embraced him and kissed him, and bade them fetch the fortune from the graveyard and give it to him, and bade them bring him support and gifts from the elder's house, a daily rate for every day, all the days of his life.

Blessed be He who maketh poor and bringeth low, who lifteth up and maketh rich, as it is written: "He raiseth up the poor out of the dust, He lifteth up the needy from the dung-hill."

CONCERNING HATRED

Jacob ben Wolf Kranz

Lithuania—Volhynia, 18th Century

FROM THE SEFER HA-MIDDOT

But you, whom God has blessed, have a care not to grieve the heart of your Lord by hating one whom he loves. For dear to him, and cherished beyond all bounds, is every man of integrity. Would you act against your brother in this way in your parents' house? If you thus rebelled against them, you would grieve the hearts of your parents and teachers. And how much more does this hold with regard to the Lord! The love of a father for his child is only a drop of water from out of the sea, compared to the love of God, blessed be he, for man. And how can you then

slander your neighbor, or raise your voice against him?
Remember: If a man does something contrary to law, the
"attribute of justice" will, to be sure, accuse him, but the
"attribute of mercy" will oppose it and try to save him.
In our case, however, the attribute of mercy, which strives
in behalf of your neighbor with all its strength, will turn
against you, and drive you from your place, as it is written:
"And it shall come to pass, when he crieth unto Me, that
I will hear; for I am gracious." Yes, the attribute of mercy
will turn into the attribute of justice with regard to you—
and upon whom did you rely, when you dared to rebel?
Therefore, do the bidding of your Lord, and love your
neighbor's life as your own, if you would be loved by God
on high, and if on this earth you would find favor among
men.

For whoever loves God's creatures is held in honor by
them. But see to it that you love your neighbor in the same
manner in which you love the people of your house, for
this love is graven in your heart. Cherish their honor and
their will to the utmost of your ability, and do their will
as though it were your own. And if your neighbor is guilty
of a blameworthy act, do not hate him for it, for this
would only prove that you did not love him before. For
if you loved him, you would be sorrowful and grieved to
hear that he has done something ugly, just as you would be
sad if they told you the like about your child or your
brother. Him you would rebuke with devotion, with
friendly words, and with none other present—as is proper
toward one you love and who lives at the very core of your
heart—and you would ask him what caused him to act as
he did, or the like. According to the words, "Thou shalt
not hate thy brother in thy heart: thou shalt surely rebuke
thy neighbor": that is to say, rebuke him with words spoken
alone, face to face with him. And if you are separated from
each other, at least you must not "bear sin because of him,"
but "in righteousness shalt thou judge thy neighbor," and
you must not condemn him until life has put you in his
position. For it is possible that in his position and with a
like cause, you yourself would act much more reprehen-
sibly than your neighbor. In no case, therefore, may you
hate him, rather shall your great love and mercy fill you

with sorrow and grief concerning the disaster that has befallen him.

But if you know in your heart that you are not peaceably disposed toward him, or that you hate him, shut your eyes, and do not look upon his failing with malicious pleasure, in order to shame him with reproof. For he who hates only follows the urge to oppress the heart of his neighbor and to rejoice in his fall. He does not consider whether he has any profit or advantage from this, or whether he destroys his soul and his life, for he only desires and lusts to rejoice in the fall of his neighbor. Therefore close your lips, lest you become sinful by giving a rebuke and destroy your soul without bettering your neighbor. God himself will send your neighbor one who is more adequate for his needs than you.

Consider the ways of the tyrants of old, of Pharaoh, of Nebuchadnezzar, and those like them, who tormented our souls. Even though all that befell came to pass according to divine will, and we deserved to suffer the evil done to us, still God's anger turned against them. And this was because they were of malicious intent, because they dealt toward us with violence in their souls and wickedness in their hearts, because they rejoiced in our suffering and desired to see sorrow upon us and burden upon our spirits. Therefore, beware of punishing your neighbor, or of hating him. And should your urge tempt you and try to convince you that it is suitable and fitting to hate a man who has committed a heinous crime—even if this were true, you would still have to ask yourself if you would rejoice in his fall, and if God would not then have to condemn your hatred and zeal, because of your malice.

But if your heart be devout, you will sorrow for the transgressor, you will pray for him and seek to re-establish him, if this is possible by the means we have indicated. If it is not possible, leave him and trust to God to do what is right in his eyes, to have mercy on him and set his feet in the right path, so that he may come to a good end, as it is written: "Yet doth he devise means that he that is banished be not an outcast from him." Seek therefore to love him for the sake of his end, for it is God's wont to credit a man with the good he will at some time do. Hatred is seemly

only when there is no hope at all that a man will at any
time regain his uprightness, either in this or in the coming
life. King David, peace be with him, also said this: "Do not
I hate them, O Lord, that hate Thee? And do not I strive
with those that rise up against Thee?" These words are
directed against rebels and blasphemers whose actions
spring from defiance, against those, therefore, concerning
whom the sages said: "Hell will pass, but they will not
pass." [1]

All in all: There is no pale in which hatred is permis-
sible, and it has not been permitted in any way, as it is
written: "Thou shalt not hate thy brother in thy heart,"
and those who may be classed in the above-mentioned
category, those whom we should hate, are actually very few.
Strive with all your might to remove hatred from your
heart, and to nurture love in your soul, according to the
words: "Thou shalt love thy neighbor as thyself." There is
no difference between this commandment and that concerning the phylacteries and the fringes in the corners of
the garment. From early youth you were brought up to
bind on phylacteries, to wear fringes, and to desist from
eating forbidden food; but in loving your neighbor as yourself, and in avoiding hatred—here the very opposite ob-
tained! For in childhood and youth it is usual to fight with
the other children in the neighborhood, and to quarrel
with them, and later on one does the same with older persons, until the habit of hating one's fellow men becomes
great and powerful and seems of slight significance to you,
because you are so accustomed to it. But why should you
forget that One Lord gave us all the commandments of
the holy Torah, and that we have no right to pull them
apart and to make distinctions!

Remember, O remember what you have torn asunder
and destroyed up to now! For because of our many sins,
this evil is very widespread among our people, who have
not become aware of the divine way—since they are too
greatly concerned with obtaining their food.

But well to him who opens his eyes and sets his mind
upon donning armor, like a soldier, to fare forth in the
battle against habit. Equip yourself for that which is good

[1] Rosh ha-Shanah 17 a.

for you in both worlds. Enrich your heart with love and
friendship, so that you love your neighbor as yourself;
wish him well, have mercy upon him in his misfortune,
and do not observe his fall with malicious pleasure, but
grieve in your heart for the sad fate that has struck him
who is like you. Make all effort in his behalf, so that you
may live to see him re-established, rejoice in his solace,
and boast of his friendship.

ON GOSSIP AND HATRED

Jonah ben Abraham Gerondi

Spain, 13th Century

FROM THE IGGERET HA-TESHUBAH

Let a man keep himself pure of pernicious gossiping, for
thus spoke our masters, blessed be their memory: Whosoever recounts pernicious gossip, is like one who denies the
divine principle,[1] for it is written: "Who have said: 'Our
tongue will we make mighty; our lips are with us: who is
lord over us?' " And likewise is a man forbidden to listen
to pernicious gossip. Thus spoke our masters, blessed be
their memory: Four groups cannot receive the Divine
Presence, and these are the group of those who scoff, the
group of those who lie, the group of those who flatter, and
the group of those who recount pernicious gossip.[2]

And let a man keep himself pure from bearing tales, as
it is written: "Thou shalt not go up and down as a tale-
bearer among thy people."

And it is man's duty to be merciful and not to narrow
his eyes in envy, as it is written: "Thou shalt not harden
thy heart, nor shut thy hand from thy needy brother."

And let a man keep himself pure of pride and arrogance,
for these are an abomination to God, as it is written:

1 Arakin 15 b.
2 Sanhedrin 103 a.

"Every one that is proud in heart is an abomination to the Lord." And it is written: "That his heart be not lifted up above his brethren." And it is written: "Then thy heart be lifted up, and thou forget the Lord thy God."

And let a man keep himself pure of hating his neighbor, as it is written: "Thou shalt not hate thy brother in thy heart." And our masters, blessed be their memory, said: The second sanctuary—there were the Torah and good works, yet why was it destroyed? Because of the groundless hatred that was among men.[1] And groundless hatred brings a man within reach of many transgressions of the Torah. Our masters, blessed be their memory, said: " 'Thou shalt love thy neighbor as thyself'—that is the essence of the Torah." [2] For through the love of one's neighbor and through peace, Israel translates the Torah into reality.

THE POOR MAN

from the Talmud and the Midrash

ADMITTANCE TO THE KING

Rabbi Dostai of the house of Yannai expounded thus:

Come and hear: The way of the Holy One, blessed be he, is not like the way of him who is of flesh and blood.

The way of him who is of flesh and blood is this: When a man brings a great gift for the king, it is uncertain if it will be accepted, or if it will not be accepted. And even if you can say that his gift will be accepted, it is still uncertain whether he may behold the king's face, or whether he may not behold the king's face.

But the Holy One, blessed be he, is not like this. When a man gives a coin to the poor, he is found worthy to receive the Divine Presence, as it is written: "I shall behold Thy face in righteousness."

1 Yoma 9 b.
2 Midrash Genesis Rabbah xxiv.

THE POORER MAN

The daughter of Kalba Sabua betrothed herself to Rabbi Akiba. Kalba Sabua heard of it and vowed that she should not enjoy a doit of his property. But in the winter she went and married Akiba. They lay down to sleep in the straw; he had to pick the straw out of his hair. He said to her: "If I had the wherewithal, I would give you a Jerusalem wrought out of gold." [1]

Elijah came to them in the guise of a mortal. He called at the door and said to them: "Give me a little straw. My wife has given birth to a child, and I have nothing on which to lay her."

Then Rabbi Akiba said to his wife: "See—there is a man who has not even straw!"

I AND HE

Said Rab Judah ben Rab Simon:
The poor man sits and grumbles:
"How am I different from that fellow? Yet he sleeps in his
   bed, and I sleep here. He sleeps in his house, and I here!"
Now if you rise and give him something,
by your life,
I shall consider it [says God]
as though you had made peace between him and Me.

GOD'S PEOPLE

Israel spoke before the Holy One, blessed be he: "Who is
   your people?"
Said he to them: "The poor! For it is written: 'For the
   Lord hath comforted His people, and hath compassion
   upon His afflicted.' "

[1] An article of jewelry worn by women.

THE DESTINY OF ISRAEL

ISRAEL

from the Talmud and the Midrash

THE BURNING BUSH

"And the angel of the Lord appeared unto him
in a flame of fire out of the midst of a bush."
A heathen asked Rabbi Joshua ben Karhah:
"Why did the Holy One, blessed be he, choose to speak
    to Moses out of the midst of a thornbush?"
The rabbi answered him:
"Had it been out of the midst of a carob tree or out of the
    midst of a sycamore, you would have asked the same
    question.
Still, I cannot send you away empty-handed.
Well then: Why out of the midst of a thornbush?
To teach you that there is no place void of the Presence
    of God, not even a thornbush!"

Rabbi Johanan said:
As one takes of the thornbush to fence in a garden,
So Israel is the fence to the world.

DUST AND STAR

"And in multiplying, I will multiply thy seed
as the stars of the heaven, and as the sand
which is upon the seashore."
This Rabbi Judah ben Ilai interpreted thus:
This people is compared to dust,

and it is compared to stars.
When it sinks,
it sinks into the very dust;
when it rises,
it rises to the very stars.

GOD CHOOSES THE OPPRESSED

Rabbi Judah ben Rabbi Simon spoke in the name of
    Rabbi Jose ben Rabbi Nehorai:
Ever does the Holy One, blessed be he, demand from the
    persecutors the blood of the persecuted.
Know that this is so,
for:

Abel was persecuted by Cain,
but the Holy One, blessed be he, chose Abel.
For it is said:
"And the Lord had respect unto Abel and to his offering,
but unto Cain and to his offering He had not respect."

Abraham was persecuted by Nimrod,
but the Holy One, blessed be he, chose Abraham.
For it is said:
"Thou art the Lord the God, who didst chose Abram."

Isaac was persecuted by the Philistines,
but the Holy One, blessed be he, chose Isaac.
For it is said:
"We saw plainly that the Lord was with thee."

Jacob was persecuted by Esau,
but the Holy One, blessed be he, chose Jacob.
For it is said:
"The Lord hath chosen Jacob unto Himself."

Moses was persecuted by Pharaoh,
but the Holy One, blessed be he, chose Moses.
For it is said:
"Had not Moses His chosen
stood before Him in the breach."

David was persecuted by Saul,
but the Holy One, blessed be he, chose David.
For it is said:
"He chose David also His servant."

Israel is persecuted by the peoples of the world,
but the Holy One, blessed be he, chose Israel.
For it is said:
"The Lord hath chosen thee to be His own treasure
out of all peoples that are upon the face of the earth."

Said Rabbi Eliezer ben Rabbi Zimri:
It is the same with the sacrifices.
The Holy One, blessed be he, said:
Cattle are pursued by the lion,
the goat is pursued by the pard,
the lamb by the wolf;
do not make sacrifice to me of the pursuers, but rather of
    those pursued.
For it is written:
"When a bullock, or a sheep, or a goat, is brought forth . . .
it may be accepted for an offering made by fire unto the
    Lord."

LIKE OIL

"Thy name is as ointment poured forth."

As oil is first bitter, but in the end sweet,
so likewise:
"Though thy beginning was small,
Yet thy end should greatly increase."

As oil cannot be improved, save that it be strained,
so likewise Israel:
It cannot turn from sin
save through suffering.

As with oil:
If you hold in your hand a cup full of oil,
and a drop of water falls therein,

a drop of oil must needs spill out.
And likewise:
If a word of the Torah enters your heart,
a scoffing word will spill out,
but if a scoffing word enters your heart,
a word of the Torah will spill out.

As oil brings light into the world,
so Israel is a light for the world,
as it is said:
"And nations shall walk at thy light,
and kings at the brightness of thy rising."

As oil is soundless,
so likewise is Israel:
it does not resound in this world.

THE NEED OF ISRAEL AND THE NEED OF PEOPLES

Rabbi Johanan said:
All distress that Israel and the peoples of the world bear
   in common
is distress;
the distress confined to Israel alone
is not distress.

Rabbi Johanan said:
In that night when Israel crossed the Red Sea,
the Divine Messengers desired to sing a song
in the presence of the Holy One, blessed be he.
But the Holy One, blessed be he, forbade it, and said
   to them:
My legions are in distress, and you would sing a song in
   my presence?

THE OPEN GATE

The Holy One, blessed be he, does not disqualify a single
   creature.
Rather,
he accepts them all.

The gates are open at all hours;
whoever would enter,
let him enter.

DOING

I call upon heaven and earth as witnesses:
Whether it be one of another faith or a Jew, whether it be
a man or a woman, whether it be a serving man or a
serving maid—
according to the deed that each does,
the spirit of holiness will rest upon him.

THE HEART OF THE NATIONS

Judah ha-Levi

Spain—Palestine, 11th—12th Century

FROM THE KUZARI

The master said: Israel is to peoples as the heart is to the
limbs. It is greater in sicknesses than all, and it is greater
than all in health.

The Chazar king said: Make this clearer to me.

The master said: The heart is constantly attacked by
sickness—by care, worry, fright, anger, hatred, love, and
dangers. Its nature suffers perpetual flux and change
through too much and too little. And besides this, bad
food and bad drink, motion, the efforts of labor, sleeping
and waking, all act upon the heart while the limbs are at
rest.

The Chazar king said: Now I clearly see in what way it
is greater in sickness than all the limbs, but make it clear
to me in what way it is greater than all in health.

The master said: Is it possible for poisonous juices to
accumulate in the heart, and for these to bring about a
swelling, a cancer, an ulcer, a wound, a loss of sensation, or
a feeling of exhaustion? For all these things are possible
if such an accumulation occurs in the limbs.

The Chazar king said: It is not possible, for death would come as a result of even much less than this. Because of the pure quality of its sensation, which follows from the purity of its blood and the greatness of its strength, the heart is enabled to feel the slightest ill that approaches it, and to throw it off as long as it has the capacity of throwing off. The other limbs are lacking in this kind of sensation, and therefore the poisonous juices can accumulate and bring about sickness.

The master said: So the heart's capacity for pain and its sensitiveness result in many sicknesses for it, but they are also the reason why, in the initial stages of these sicknesses, before they have time to take root, the heart can throw them off.

The Chazar king said: That is the way it is.

The master said: The relation of the divine to us is as the relation of soul to heart. And therefore it is said: "You only have I known of all the families of the earth, therefore I will visit upon you all your iniquities." Those are the sicknesses. But what our masters said of health is this: "He forgives the iniquities of his people, of Israel, by always obliterating the former." [1] Thus he does not allow iniquities to accumulate within us, and so cause utter destruction, as he did in the case of the Amorite, of whom it is said: "For the iniquity of the Amorite is not yet full." God let him go his ways until the sickness of his iniquities was so great that it resulted in death. And just as the heart, in its very root and nature, is of such harmony in its blending that the power of life is bound up with it, thus is it also with Israel, with its root and its nature. And as the heart is attacked by sickness by way of the other parts of the body, by way of the greeds of the liver and of the stomach, as a result of the poor mixing of juices—so Israel is attacked by sickness because of its mingling with other peoples, as it is said: "But mingled themselves with the nations and learned their works." And so it must not seem strange to you that it is written: "Surely diseases he did bear and our pains he carried." [2] Thus we are in distress,

[1] From the prayers for fast days and the Ten Days of Turning.
[2] Referring to the suffering servant of God, who is understood to be Israel.

the world is at peace. But the distress that strikes us is meant to keep our faith firm, to cleanse us completely, and to cast out the dross from our midst. Through what we have that is clear and upright, the divine is connected with the world. You know that the elements originated so that minerals could originate from them, and then plants, and then animals, and then men, and finally the elect among men. All that was created was for the sake of these elect, so that the divine might inhabit them. But these elect originated for the sake of the most elect, of the prophets and the devout.

THE SURVIVAL OF ISRAEL

Moses Maimonides

Spain—Egypt, 12th Century

FROM HIS EPISTLE TO THE JEWS IN YEMEN, 1172 [1]

The antagonism of the nations toward us is due to our unique position as a people of faith. This is why their kings oppress us, to visit upon us hatred and hostility. But the Creator endowed us with confidence, so that whenever persecution or fury against Israel arises, it will surely be endured. The power of the kings presses down upon us and they exercise a hard rule over us; they persecute and torment us with oppressive decrees, but they cannot destroy us or wipe out our name.

Do you not know, brethren, that in the time of the wicked Nebuchadnezzar, Israel was forced to worship foreign gods, and only Daniel, Hananiah, Mishael, and Azariah were rescued? But in the end, this king and his authority were destroyed and truth was restored. The same

1 The Jews of Yemen in southern Arabia were compelled to choose between accepting Islam or suffering persecution and expulsion. In addition, a pseudomessianic movement created confusion within the community. Jacob al Fayumi, a representative of the Jews who opposed the false messiah, turned to Maimonides for counsel. The Epistle to the Jews of Yemen was Maimonides' answer.

happened in the time of the Second Temple, when the wicked dynasty of Seleucus came into power and persecuted Israel in order to destroy its religion. The Syrians forced Israel to desecrate the Sabbath and the covenant of circumcision and publicly to renounce belief in God. This oppression lasted fifty-two years, and then God annihilated both the government and the religion of the enemy.

God promised us through his prophets that we shall never perish and that we shall never cease to be a nation of faith. Our life is correlated with the existence of the Lord. As it is said: "For I the Lord change not, therefore ye, O sons of Jacob, are not consumed." And Moses, our teacher, said in the Torah: "And yet for all that, when they are in the land of their enemies, I will not reject them, neither will I abhor them, to destroy them and to break My covenant with them; for I am the Lord their God."

Therefore, brethren, be strong and of good courage. If persecutions arise, let them not disconcert you. Let not the mighty hand of the enemy and the weakness of our nation frighten you. These events are but trial and proof of your faith and your love. By holding firm to the law of truth in times like these, you prove that you belong to those of Jacob's seed who fear God and who are named "the remnant whom the Lord shall call."

It is your duty, our brethren of Israel, who are scattered over the whole earth, to strengthen one another. The older should encourage the younger, and the prominent men the multitude. The nation should be united in the name of truth, which does not change. Raise your voice in strong faith, proclaiming to all that God is One, that Moses is his prophet and the greatest of all the prophets, that the Torah is the word of the Creator. Keep ever in mind the event on Mount Sinai.

My brethren, rear your children to understand that great event; expound to every group and community its significance. The event on Mount Sinai is the pivot on which our faith turns, the foundation that leads us to the truth. Understand, my brethren, the meaning of that covenant: the nation as a whole witnessed the word of God and His presence. This event should strengthen our faith and enable us to resist the strain of persecutions and intolerance in times like these. It is said: "God is come to prove you, and that His fear may be before you, that ye sin not." This is to say, that experience should give you strength to withstand all trials to which we may be subjected in times to come. Therefore, brethren, hold fast to the covenant and be steadfast in your faith.

THE ASCENDING FLAME

from the Zohar

Spain, 13th Century

Rabbi Simeon said: "I have still one thing more to tell you. It says in one place, 'For the Lord thy God is a consuming fire,' and in another place, 'And ye that cleave to the Lord your God are all of you alive this day.' The apparent contradiction between these texts has already been discussed among the colleagues, but here is another explanation.

"It has already been established among the colleagues that there is a fire which consumes fire and destroys it, because there is one sort of fire stronger than another. Pursuing this idea, we may say that he who desires to penetrate to the mystery of the holy unity should contemplate the flame that rises from a burning coal or candle.

"The flame cannot rise save from some concrete body. Further, in the flame itself there are two lights, one white and luminous, and the other black or blue. The white light is the higher of the two and rises steadily. The black or blue light is underneath the other, which rests upon it as upon a pedestal. The two are inseparably connected, the white resting and being enthroned upon the black. This blue or black base is, in turn, attached to something beneath it that keeps it burning and impels it to cling to the white light above. This blue or black light sometimes turns red, but the white light above never changes its color. The lower light, which is sometimes black, sometimes blue, and sometimes red, is a connecting link between the white light to which it is attached above and the concrete body to which it is attached below, and which keeps it alight. This light always consumes anything that is under it or that is brought in contact with it, for it is its nature to be a source of destruction and death. But the white light that is above it never consumes or destroys and never changes.

"Therefore Moses said: 'For the Lord thy God is a consuming fire,' literally consuming all that is beneath him; that is why he said 'thy God' and not 'our God,' because Moses was in that white light above which does not consume or destroy.

"Now observe: The impulse through which this light is set aflame and attaches itself to the white light comes from Israel, who cleave to it from below. Further, although it is the nature of this blue or black light to consume everything that is in contact with it beneath, Israel is nevertheless able to cleave to it from below and still exist; so it is written: 'And ye that cleave to the Lord your God are all of you alive this day.' 'Your God' and not 'our God'— namely, that blue or black flame which consumes and destroys all that cleaves to it from below: yet you cleave and are still alive.

"Above the white light, and surrounding it, is still another light, scarcely perceptible, which symbolizes the supreme essence. Thus the ascending flame symbolizes the highest mysteries of wisdom. . . ."

Rabbi Phinehas approached and kissed him, saying: "Blessed be God who led my steps here."

They then accompanied Rabbi Phinehas three miles upon his way.

THE PROSELYTE

Moses Maimonides

Spain—Egypt, 12th Century

A RESPONSUM

I received the question of the wise scholar, Obadiah the proselyte. You ask as to whether you, being a proselyte, should utter the prayers: "Our God and God of *our fathers;* Who has separated *us* from the nations; Who has brought *us* out of Egypt."[1]

Pronounce all prayers as they are written and do not change anything. Your prayer and blessing should be the same as that of any other Israelite, regardless of whether you pray in private or conduct the service. The explanation is as follows: Abraham, our father, taught mankind the true belief and the unity of God, repudiating idolatry; through him many of his own household and also others were guided "to keep the way of the Lord, to do righteousness and justice." Thus he who becomes a proselyte and confesses the unity of God, as taught in the Torah, is a disciple of Abraham, our father. Such persons are of his household. Just as Abraham influenced his contemporaries through his word and teaching, so he leads to belief all future generations, through the testament he gave to his children and his household. In this sense Abraham is the father of his descendants who follow his ways, and of his disciples, and of all the proselytes.

You should therefore pray, "Our God and God of our fathers," for Abraham is also *your* father. In no respect is there a difference between us and you. And certainly you should say, "Who has given unto *us* the law,"· because the law was given to us and the proselytes alike, as it is said: "As for the congregation, there shall be one statute both for you and for the stranger [2] who lives with you; as ye are, so shall the stranger be before the Lord. One law

---

[1] Since his fathers were non-Jews.
[2] Hebrew *ger.* Later this word assumed the meaning "proselyte."

and one ordinance shall be both for you and for the stranger that lives with you." Keep in mind that most of our ancestors who left Egypt were idol worshipers; they mingled with the Egyptian heathen and imitated their ways, until God sent Moses, our teacher, the master of all the prophets. He separated us from these nations, initiated us into the belief in God, us and all the proselytes, and gave us one law.

Do not think little of your origin: we are descended from Abraham, Isaac, and Jacob, but your descent is from the Creator, for in the words of Isaiah, "One shall say: 'I am the Lord's'; and another shall call himself by the name of Jacob."

THE PARABLE OF THE SEED

Judah ha-Levi

Spain—Palestine, 11th–12th Century

FROM THE KUZARI

The Chazar king said: The light of which you speak has been dimmed to such a point that it is hardly conceivable that it will ever wax great again. It is so far lost that the thought of its restoration can hardly be entertained any longer.

The master said: It appears to be extinguished only to those who do not see us with vision unblurred and to those who argue from our degradation, poverty, and dispersion that our light has been quenched, and who likewise argue from the lofty state of the other nations, from their worldly attainments, and from their rule over us that their light is still burning.

The Chazar king said: I did not base my argument upon this, for I observe that of the two antagonistic religions each has greatness of power, although it cannot be that the truth lies with both of two opposites; it must lie only with one or with neither of them. You have already explained the words, "Behold, My servant shall prosper," as meaning that humility and meekness are nearer to the Divine Influence than greatness and pride. Furthermore, it is evident in the case of the two religions that the Christians do not glory in kings, or in men of valor, or in men of wealth, but rather in those who followed Jesus throughout all those many days when that faith had not yet taken firm root among them. And these men wandered about in exile, or hid away, or were done to death wherever they were found, and suffered untold dishonor and slaughter for the preservation of their faith. It is they whom the Christians invoke in their blessings. The places in which they moved and where they were killed are revered, and churches are built in their names. In the same way did the "helpers" [1] of the early adherents of Islam suffer great dishonor until they found aid. It is in their humility, in their readiness to die in championing their faith, that they glory—not in their rulers who boasted of their wealth and of the loftiness of their estate, but rather in those who clad themselves in rags, who fed on barley bread, though not to satiety, and who did all this out of complete self-dedication to God. Were I to see the Jews do the same for the sake of their God, I would say that they deserved to be set even above the royal house of David. For I well remember what you taught me with reference to the verse, "With him also that is of a contrite and humble spirit"— that the light of God rests only upon the souls of the humble.

The master said: You are fully justified in casting upon us the blame for the exile we are suffering without benefit. Yet I am thinking of those prominent men among us who could shed that shame and bondage by a word easily spoken, and who could then become free men and even rule over those who have enslaved them—yet they do not do so, only because they are zealous to preserve their faith. Is not this devotion enough to bring intercession for and remission of many sins? If what you demand of us were ever to take place, we should not long remain in this exile. Besides, God has a secret and wise design concerning us, which may be likened to the wisdom in the minute seed

1 The men of Medina who embraced Islam in the days of Mohammed.

that falls into the ground and to all appearances is changed
and transformed into earth, water, and dirt, retaining none
of its perceptible qualities—or so it would seem to the
ordinary observer—whereas actually it is the seed that
transforms the earth and the water into its own substance.
It transmutes them little by little until it refines the elements and assimilates them to its own form, casting off
husks, leaves, etc. And once the pure core appears and is
ready to assume the Divine Influence and the form of the
first seed, then that tree produces fruit like that from which
its own seed has come. So it is in the case of the law of
Moses. All who came after it will yet be brought around
to it by virtue of its essential truth, although to all appearances they would seem to reject it. The nations serve
merely as a preamble and introduction to the awaited
Messiah, who is the fruition. And they will all become his
fruit once they acknowledge him, and the tree will be one.
Then they will glorify and revere the root that they formerly despised, as we have said—"Behold, My servant shall
prosper."

SUFFERING AND MARTYRDOM

"TO DIE AS FREE MEN!" ELEAZAR'S SPEECH
AT MASADA

Flavius Josephus

Palestine—Rome, 1st-2d Century

FROM BELLUM JUDAICUM

But Eleazar [1] did not dream of flight, nor would he have permitted anyone else to flee. Quite the contrary! When he saw the walls destroyed by fire, and could think of no other means to save or defend, he conjured up before his eyes the treatment the women and children would suffer if they fell into the hands of the Romans, and came to the conclusion that all must seek death. And since, as matters stood, he considered this best, he called together the staunchest of his comrades and tried to kindle them to action with these words:

"It is long since we, my brave comrades, decided that we would be subject neither to the Romans nor to anyone else, and only to God, for he is the true and proper sovereign over men. But now we are faced with a moment that bids us translate our noble resolve into deed. We have never been able to endure even undangerous servitude, so let us not now dishonor ourselves by voluntarily submitting to servitude with the terrible torments that indubitably await us if we fall alive into the hands of the Romans. For just as

1 Leader of the host that defended Masada, the last fortress remaining to the Jews after the fall of Jerusalem (73 c.e.).

we were the very first to rebel against their yoke, so we are the last against whom they are still striving. I regard it as a special grace of God that he has put us in a position to die honorably, as free people—a death not vouchsafed to those others who were taken unawares. We know in advance that tomorrow we shall fall into the enemy's hands; but we still have the free choice of dying a noble death together with our loved ones. Our enemies cannot prevent us from doing this, even though they would very much like to get us into their power alive. On the other hand, we are no longer able to vanquish them in battle. In the very beginning, perhaps, when our striving for freedom met with such great resistance on the part of our own people, and still more on that of our foes, we should have divined and recognized God's decision to dedicate to destruction the Jewish people that once was so dear to him. For had he remained gracious toward us, or moderated his wrath, he would not have looked on quietly while so many perished, and would not have yielded his holy city up to fire and to our enemies' ravening thirst for destruction. And do we—in spite of this—venture to hope that we could survive, we of all the Jewish people, and save our freedom, as though we had not sinned against God, nor participated in transgressions, while actually in this we were those who taught the others? You see how God is giving the lie to our idle expectations, by permitting a calamity to come upon us that utterly shatters our hopes.

"For in what way has this invincible fortress aided us in our salvation? And did not God himself take from us all hope of being saved, although we had rich stores of supplies, an abundance of arms, and all other necessary things in profusion? For it was not sheer chance that directed to the wall we had set up the fire that was first turned against the enemy, but rather the wrath of God for the many crimes we in our madness committed against our own people. But we want to suffer our punishment for this not from our deadly enemies, from the Romans, but from God, through the act of our own hands; for his judgment is more merciful. Let our wives die undisgraced, and our children free from the shackles of slavery! And after they have preceded us in death, let us perform a service of love for one another, and then the glory of having sustained freedom will take the place of an honorable burial. But first let us destroy our treasures and the entire fortress with fire. For I am certain the Romans will be enraged if they are unable to catch us alive, and lose the loot into the bargain. We shall leave nothing for them but our provisions, so that when we are dead these may bear testimony that it was not hunger that vanquished us, but that, just as in the beginning, so now too we were resolved to prefer death to slavery. . . .

"No, as long as these hands are free and able to hold the sword, they shall do us the best possible service! We shall die unsubjugated by our enemies; we shall depart this life as free men, we and our women and children. That is what our laws bid us do; that is what our women and children plead for. But it is God himself who has made it necessary for us to take this step, and the wish of the Romans is exactly opposed to it: they are afraid that one of us might die before the fall of the fortress. Therefore, let us make haste, so that instead of the happiness they hope for, the happiness of capturing us, we leave behind for them the horrible spectacle of our bodies, and amazement at our valor."

And none proved too weak for this dreadful task; all killed their loved ones, one after another. Oh, what terrible adversity, that caused these unhappy people to regard the slaughtering of their women and children with their own hands as the lesser evil! Incapable of enduring their grief at their own deed, and in the feeling that it would be wronging the dead to survive them for even a short while, they hurriedly made a heap of all their valuables, set it afire, and thereupon chose by lot ten of their number to dispatch the rest. Stretched at the side of his wife and his children, and spreading his arms over them, each willingly exposed his throat to the ten who performed the sad service. But scarcely had these last slaughtered all their comrades without hesitation or tremor, when they drew lots for the same procedure with respect to themselves. He on whom the lot fell, was to kill the other nine, and finally himself, for they had firm confidence regarding one another that each would joyfully submit to the execution of the decision, whether in an active or passive role.

Thus the nine suffered death by the sword. But the one who remained, the last to be alive, examined the mass of bodies to see whether any had been left out in this vast slaughter and required his help to die. When he found that they were all with certainty dead, he set fire to the palace, stabbed himself with unwavering hand, and sank down beside his family. The dead numbered nine hundred and sixty, including women and children.[1]

THE TEN MARTYRS [2]

from the Talmud and the Midrash

RABBI SIMEON BEN GAMALIEL AND RABBI ISHMAEL

"And a stranger shalt thou not wrong, neither shalt thou oppress him. Ye shall not afflict any widow, or fatherless child. If thou afflict them in any wise—for if they cry at all unto Me, I will surely hear their cry."

Rabbi Ishmael and Rabbi Simeon were on the way to their execution.

Rabbi Simeon said to Rabbi Ishmael: "Rabbi, my heart is consumed, for I do not know why I am to be executed."

Rabbi Ishmael said to Rabbi Simeon: "Perhaps a man once came to you to hear judgment, or to consult you about something, and you let him wait until you had emptied your goblet, or fastened your sandals, or put on your cloak? The Torah says: 'If thou afflict them in any wise.' It counts the same whether you afflict them greatly or only a little!"

1 Josephus then tells of two women and five children who were left in the aqueducts and survived the tragedy of Masada.

2 Jewish tradition speaks of ten great teachers who suffered death for their faith in the period of persecution under Hadrian after the end of the revolt of Bar Kokba (132–135 C.E.).

Then the other said to him: "You have consoled me, Rabbi!"

A highborn Roman matron fastened her gaze upon Ishmael, for he was a man of great beauty, and in this he was like Joseph, the son of Jacob. She said to the executioners: "Tell him to raise his head, so that I can see him; I shall grant him his life."

But he did not heed her request. When she repeated the same thing a second and a third time, Ishmael answered: "Shall I forfeit the bliss of eternal life for an hour of pleasures such as those!"

When the godless woman heard this answer, she said to the executioners: "Flay him!"

They went to work. They began at his chin and flayed the skin of the righteous from his face. When they came to his forehead, to the place where the phylacteries are fastened, Ishmael uttered a piercing scream that shook the earth, and cried: "Lord of the world, will you not have mercy upon me?"

A voice from heaven answered him: "If you accept the suffering to which you have been sentenced, it is well; if not, I shall let the world lapse back into chaos."

Then Ishmael willingly suffered martyrdom.

RABBI AKIBA

"And thou shalt love the Lord thy God with all thy heart, and with all thy soul, and with all thy might."

Rabbi Akiba taught: " 'With all thy soul'—that means: You shall love God even in that hour in which he takes your soul from you."

When Akiba was led off to be executed—it was the hour in which "Hear, O Israel" is recited—they gashed his flesh with iron combs, but he willingly took the punishment of heaven upon himself. When he avowed his faith, he drew out the last word, which testifies that God is One, and the breath of life left him while he was saying the word "One."

Then a voice sounded from heaven: "Hail to you, Akiba, whose last breath was spent upon the word 'One.' "

The Messengers said to God: "Such is the Torah, and
such is its reward? Is it not written: 'To die by Thy
hand, O Lord'—'thy hand,' but not the hand of man?"
Then he answered them: "Their portion is . . . life!"
And a voice rang out: "Blessed be you, Akiba, you who
have been elected to life in the coming world!"

"Gather My saints, those that have made a covenant
with Me by sacrifice." The "saints"—those are the righteous
whom every age brings forth. "Those that have made a
covenant" are, above all, the three in the fiery furnace—
Hananiah, Mishael, and Azariah. And the "sacrifice" refers
to Akiba and his friends, who were willing to let themselves be slaughtered for the sake of the Torah.

RABBI JUDAH BEN BABA

The memory of the man whose name is Judah ben Baba
is held in high honor. Had it not been for him, Israel
would have forgotten the laws regarding penalty.

Once the wicked empire of Rome had a devastating law
proclaimed, to the effect that ordination of scholars would
no longer be permitted. The master who laid his hands
upon his disciple and ordained him was to be executed,
likewise the disciple who submitted to the laying on of
hands on the part of his master. A city in which such an
act took place was to be destroyed, and everything within
the bounds of the place in which it occurred, torn down.

What did Rabbi Judah ben Baba do? He went to a place
flanked on two sides by high mountains, and equally distant from two great cities, between the Sabbath bounds
of the cities of Usha and Shefaram.[1] There he himself ordained five to teacherhood—Rabbi Meir, Rabbi Judah,
Rabbi Simeon, Rabbi Jose, and Rabbi Eleazar ben Shammua; and some say that Rabbi Nehemiah was also included.

When their enemies discovered them, Rabbi Judah ben
Baba said to the five: "My sons, flee!"
They said: "But master, what will become of you?"

[1] By his selection of this place, no city would suffer.

He replied: "I shall lie here before them as if I were a stone that none cares to move."

It is told that the enemy did not leave that place until three hundred lances had pierced Rabbi Judah, and his body was like a sieve.

RABBI HANINA BEN TERADION

About Hanina ben Teradion they relate that he was in the act of reading the Torah when the bailiffs came to fetch him. When they found him deep in his book, they said: "Have you not been sentenced to be burned to death?"

He answered them, saying: " 'The Rock, His work is perfect: for all His ways are justice.' "

Hanina's wife asked him: "What is to be my fate?"

He answered her: "Death by the sword."

Thereupon she said: " 'A God of faithfulness and without iniquity, just and right is He.' "

Hanina's daughter asked him: "And what has been decreed for me?"

His answer was: "Your father has been condemned to burn to death, your mother to be slain; you, however, will be forced to sit in a house of harlots."

Then she cried out: " 'The Lord of hosts, great in counsel, and mighty in work'!"

How holy were these three people, the master, his wife, and his daughter—in the very hour when they had to submit to the judgment of heaven, they thought of three verses in the Scriptures that deal with justice and the judgment of God!

They relate:

When Hanina was led away to be burned to death, his daughter wept. He asked her: "Daughter, why do you weep?"

She answered him: "I weep for the Torah that is to be burned with you."

He answered: "The Torah is fire, and no fire can burn fire itself."

They seized him and wrapped him in the scroll of the Torah, heaped faggots around him, and lit the pyre. But they took woolen cloths, soaked them in water, and laid them on his heart, so that he should not die too quickly.

His disciples said: "Rabbi, what do you see?"

He replied: "I see the parchment consumed by fire, but the letters of the Scriptures are flying aloft."

They continued: "Rabbi, open your mouth wide, that the fire may enter more swiftly."

He said: "It is better that only He who gave the soul should take it, rather than that men do anything to hasten it on its way."

Then the executioner said to Rabbi Hanina: "If I quicken the flames and take the cooling cloth from your heart—will you bring me into eternal life?"

The martyr answered: "That I will do."

The Roman went on: "Swear it."

And Rabbi Hanina gave him his oath. At once the executioner quickened the flames, took the woolen cloths from the teacher's heart, and soon after, his soul left his body. But the executioner threw himself into the fire.

Then a voice sounded from heaven, and called: "Hanina ben Teradion and the Roman executioner are both chosen for the life in the world to come!"

Concerning this event, Rabbi Judah the Prince once said with tears: "One man can win eternal life in an hour, while another needs many years."

HUZPIT, THE INTERPRETER

Then Huzpit, the interpreter, was to be put to death. He was a very old man—a hundred and thirty years old— beautiful in face and form, and like one of God's angels. They told the emperor of his great age and of his beauty, and begged him to show mercy to this one man.

The emperor turned to the condemned and asked him: "What is your age?"

Huzpit replied: "One hundred and thirty years less one day, and I beg of you to give me this one day."

The emperor said: "What difference does it make whether you die today or tomorrow?"

The old man answered: "There are two commandments

that I should like to carry out one more time. I want to recite 'Hear, O Israel' this evening and tomorrow morning, so that once more I may avow the almighty and awful God as my king."

The emperor said: "You people who are bold in your manners and bold of spirit, how long will you continue to cling to your God who has not the power to help you?"

When Rabbi Huzpit heard these words, he wept bitterly and clutched his clothes to rend them, because of his anguish in hearing the name of the Lord blasphemed in this way. He addressed the emperor: "Woe to you, O prince! What will you do on the Day of Judgment, when the Lord punishes Rome and your gods!"

Then the emperor said: "How long am I to dally words with this old man?" And he bade them slay him with the sword, stone him, and hang him.

YESHEBAB, THE SCRIBE

Concerning Yeshebab, the scribe, they relate that he was ninety on the day he was to be executed.

His disciples asked him: "What is to become of us?"

Their teacher answered: "Cleave to one another, love peace and justice; perhaps there is hope."

They say that the day on which this holy man was killed, was the second day of the week, the day on which he usually fasted.

His pupils asked him whether he did not wish to strengthen himself with food before he died.

He answered them: "Should the servant not be content to be like his master? Should I not be content to resemble my master Judah ben Baba? He died fasting, and so I too shall do."

And the godless Roman bade them kill the devout man just as he was about to recite "Hear, O Israel." At the words, "And the Lord spoke unto Moses," he gave up the ghost.

A voice was heard and it cried: "Blessed be you, Rabbi Yeshebab, who never for an instant faltered from the law of Moses!"

RABBI HANINA BEN HAKINAI

The day on which Hanina ben Hakinai was to be executed, was the day of preparation for the Sabbath.

He began to pronounce the benediction ushering in the holy day, and got as far as the words, "And God . . . hallowed it—" but he had not finished speaking when he was killed.

A voice issued from heaven and cried: "Happy are you, Hanina, son of Hakinai, who were yourself a holy man, and whose soul flew on high at the word 'hallowed'!"

RABBI JUDAH BEN DAMA

Then it was the turn of the teacher, Judah ben Dama, to suffer punishment. But the day on which he was to be executed was the day before the Feast of Tabernacles, and so the devout man said to the emperor: "By your life, wait a little until I have blessed this holiday and praised God, who gave us the Torah."

The ruler said: "So even now you still cling to the belief that there is a God who gave you the Torah?"

The son of Dama said: "Yes."

The emperor scoffed and said: "And what reward does your faith promise you?"

Judah replied in the words of the singer of the psalms: " 'Oh, how abundant is Thy goodness, which Thou hast laid up for them that fear Thee.' "

The emperor said: "There are no fools greater than you who believe in a life after death."

To this Rabbi Judah replied: "There are no fools greater than you who deny the living God. Oh, how shamed and dishonored you will be when you see us, God's people, walking in the light of life, while you thirst in the deepest abyss!"

When he heard these words, the emperor's anger flared up. He commanded the teacher to be tied by the hair to a horse's tail and dragged through the streets of Rome, and after this he was to be torn to pieces besides.

RABBI ELEAZAR BEN SHAMMUA

Eleazar ben Shammua was the last to suffer death. He was a hundred and five years old, and no one had ever heard of his occupying himself with useless matters, or quarreling with his friends, even though his views differed from theirs. Eleazar ben Shammua was of a gentle and humble spirit, and had spent eighty years of his life fasting. The day on which he was to be executed was the Day of Atonement.

His disciples asked him: "Tell us what your eyes behold!"

He answered: "I see Rabbi Judah ben Baba borne in a litter, and beside him Akiba's litter is floating through the heavens, and they are conversing about questions in the Torah."

The disciples asked: "And who settles their disputes?"

Eleazar replied: "It is Ismael, the high priest, who is their arbiter."

And again the youths asked: "And which of them is victor in the dispute?"

Their teacher answered them: "Akiba, who while he was alive devoted himself to the Torah with all his powers." And he continued: "My sons, I see the soul of every righteous man cleansing itself in the well of Siloah, so that it may be purified for entering the school of heaven, where Akiba will teach. And the angels bring golden chairs for the righteous, who seat themselves upon them in purity."

After these words, the emperor bade them execute this devout man.

A voice was heard. It called: "Hail to you, Eleazar ben Shammua, you who have been pure, and whose soul has risen from the body in a state of purity!"

PERSECUTIONS AT THE TIME OF THE FIRST CRUSADE

Solomon ben Sampson

Germany, 12th Century

THE EVENTS AND THEIR MEANING

And now I shall relate how disaster stormed through the other congregations that submitted to slaughter for the sake of His name, for the One God, and how they clung to the Lord God of their fathers, and avowed his unity until their souls were forced from their bodies.

It was in the year 4856 [1096], in the ten hundred and twenty-eighth year of our exile, at a time when we were hoping for liberation and comfort in accordance with the prophecy of Jeremiah. But our hopes turned to griefs and sighs, to weeping and groaning, and all the calamities that all the exhortations predict, befell us; that which is written and that which is unwritten passed over our souls.

First insolent faces appeared, "a people of strange language," the bitter and violent peoples of the French and the German lands. They had set their hearts on going to the holy city that a nefarious nation had desecrated, because they wished to seek out the grave of the Nazarene, to drive from it the Ismaelites, who inhabited that land, and to subject the country by force to their own control. "They have set up their own signs for signs"; to their garments they fastened the cross—every man and woman of them whose heart bade him go on the false pilgrimage to the grave of their Anointed, until they were more numerous than the locusts on earth—men, and women, and children. And when, in the course of their journey, they came through towns in which there were Jews, they said, one to the other: "See, we are going to a faraway place, to seek out the grave of the Anointed, and take revenge upon the Ismaelites, and right among us are the Jews, whose fathers killed him, crucified him, without cause! Let us take revenge on them first; let us blot them out from among peoples! Let the name of Israel be remembered no more, or else let them avow the Nazarene as we do."

When the congregations heard such talk, they took recourse to the way of our fathers—repentance, prayer, and good works. But at that time the hands of the holy people grew slack, their hearts melted within them, their strength failed. In their innermost chambers they hid from the roving sword, and harried their souls with fasting. Three days in succession they fasted, day and night, and they fasted on many another day besides, until "their skin shrivelled upon their bones, and was withered and become like a stick." They cried, they sent forth a great and bitter cry, but their Father did not answer them, he shut out their prayer, he covered himself with a cloud, so that the prayer might not pass through. Their tent was spurned, and he put them away from him. For he himself had passed sentence that all this was to come upon them, from the time he said: "In the day when I visit, I will visit their sin upon them"; [1] and he had chosen this generation to be his portion, for it had the strength and steadfastness to stand in his halls, to do his word, and to sanctify his great name in his world. Of them David said: "Bless the Lord, ye angels of His, ye mighty in strength, that fulfil His word, hearkening unto the voice of His word."

HEAR, O ISRAEL . . .

There was a man who was devout and just, one of the great men of our time, our teacher, Rabbi Menahem, son of Rabbi Judah. He spoke into the ears of the people, and expounded to them:

Just as the sons of Jacob, our father, did when he wanted to reveal to them the end of days, and the Divine Presence left him, and he said, "Perhaps there is an unworthy one among my children, as in the case of my father Isaac, who begot an unworthy son?" and they replied, "Hear, O Israel: the Lord our God, the Lord is One," [2] and as our

[1] According to the tradition, these words, spoken after the sin of the golden calf, mean that atonement for this sin must be made through all time.

[2] Pesahim 56 a.

fathers did at the time they received the Torah on Mount Sinai and said, "All that the Lord hath spoken will we do, and obey," and raised their voices in answer, " 'Hear, O Israel: the Lord our God, the Lord is One' "—thus you shall do today.

Then they avowed his unity with a whole heart, and did as the master had bidden, and cried with one voice and with one heart: "Hear, O Israel: the Lord our God, the Lord is One."

SANCTIFICATION

When the sons of the holy covenant saw that disaster would surely come, that their enemies would vanquish them and enter their courts, they cried out, all together, old men and youths, virgins and infants, men and women servants— cried out to their Father in heaven, and wept for themselves and their lives. They accepted the judgment of heaven as a just judgment, took it upon themselves, and said, one to the other: "Let us be strong and suffer the yoke of holy reverence. For the span of an hour, our enemies will kill us, and by the easiest form of death—death by the sword. But our souls will live forever and persist in the Garden of Eden, in the great and clear vision, in all eternity."

And they spoke with whole heart and willing soul: "This is the ultimate meaning—not to ponder over the ways of the Holy One, blessed be he, and blessed be his name. He has given us his Torah, and the commandment to let ourselves be slaughtered, to die for the unity of his holy name. Happy we, if we do his will. Happy he who is killed, who is slaughtered, who dies for the name of the one God. For he is destined for the coming world and will dwell in the group of the just, with Rabbi Akiba and his friends, the fundaments of the world, who were slain for His name. And not only this! He will exchange a world of darkness for a world of light, a world of cares for a world of joys, a world that passes for a world that endures forever and ever."

Then they all cried out in a loud voice, and spoke as a single man: "We must no longer hesitate, for our enemies are already upon us. Let us go and do it quickly; let us

sacrifice ourselves before God. Every one who has a knife
shall examine it, lest it be defective, and come and slaughter us for the sanctification of the one God, of him who
lives forever, and then slaughter himself by cutting his
throat, or by stabbing his body with the knife."

NO!

And when the sons of the holy covenant lay in their chambers, the wounded and the dead, their enemies fell upon
them, to disrobe the bodies and clear them out of the
houses. They cast them from the windows naked, cast them
upon the ground heap upon heap, mound on mound,
until there was a high hill.

And many among them were still living when they were
cast from the windows, and their souls were still bound to
their bodies; a small residue of life was in them, and they
signed with their fingers to be given a little water.

And when their deluded enemies saw that a small residue
of life was still within them, they asked: "Will you let
yourselves be baptized? For then we shall give you water
to drink, and you may still be saved."

But they shook their heads, gazed up to their Father
in heaven as though they were saying "No!" and with their
fingers pointed to heaven, to the Holy One, blessed be he,
but they could utter no word with their lips because of
the many wounds they had received.

And those others continued to beat them, above these
stripes with many stripes, until they were dead twice over.

HALLOWING THE NAME OF GOD

Moses Maimonides

Spain—Egypt, 12th Century

FROM THE MISHNEH TORAH

The entire house of Israel has been commanded to hallow
God's great name, as it is written, "I will be hallowed

among the children of Israel," and not to profane it, as it is written, "And ye shall not profane My holy name." How shall we interpret this? Should an idolator arise and force a member of Israel to transgress one of all the commandments given in the Torah, and threaten to slay him if he does not, then he shall transgress and not suffer death. For it is written concerning the commandments: "Which if a man do, he shall live by them"—live by them, not that he shall die by them! But if a man dies rather than to transgress, such a one becomes responsible for his own death.

These words apply to all the commandments save only those regarding idolatry, incest, and the shedding of blood. The following governs these transgressions. If the idolator says to him, "Transgress one of these, or you will be slain," he shall die and not transgress. This distinction is valid when the idolator's purpose is his own satisfaction, as when he wants to force a man to build his house on a Sabbath, or cook his food, or when he wants to force a woman to yield to him, or the like. But if the idolator is intent solely upon having him transgress a commandment, then the following holds. If he is alone with the idolator, if ten men of Israel are not present, he shall transgress and shall not die. But if the idolator forces him to transgress while ten men of Israel are present, he shall die and not transgress, even if the idolator merely wishes him to transgress one of the remaining commandments.

All this holds for times other than the hour of religious persecution. But in the hour of persecution, that is, when a malicious king such as Nebuchadnezzar, or another like him, arises and issues decrees against Israel in order to vitiate their law or one of the commandments, then a man shall suffer death and not transgress, even if it is question of one of the remaining commandments, no matter whether he is constrained in the presence of ten or while he is alone with the idolator.

Every man for whom the words "He shall transgress and not suffer death" hold, but who, notwithstanding, does not transgress but dies—such a man becomes responsible for his own death. But every man for whom the words "He shall suffer death and not transgress" hold, and he has suffered death rather than to transgress—such a man has

hallowed the name of God, and if he did this before ten
of Israel, he has hallowed the name of God publicly, like
Daniel, Hananiah, Mishael, and Azariah, and like Rabbi
Akiba and his friends. These are the martyrs, and none
attained a higher rung than they. It is they of whom it is
written: "Nay, but for thy sake are we killed all the day;
we are accounted as sheep for the slaughter." It is they of
whom it is written: "Gather My saints together unto Me;
those that have made a covenant with Me by sacrifice."

EMIGRATION

Moses Maimonides

Spain—Egypt, 12th Century

A MESSAGE TO THE JEWS OF MOROCCO, 1160

My counsel, and the view I express with regard to myself
and my friends, and everyone who asks my advice, is that
we should leave these regions and move to where we can
fulfill the law and keep the commandments of the Torah,
without violent interference with our faith. We must not
fear to leave our houses, our children, and our possessions,
for the law of God that he gave us as a heritage is great,
and our duty toward it must take precedence over all things
accidental, which must appear but slight in the eyes of
sages, for they do not endure, while the fear of God does.
Further, if one of two Jewish cities is better in deeds and
conduct and more conscientious and devoted to the commandments than the other, a God-fearing man is duty
bound to leave the city where deeds are not quite as they
should be, and to move into the better city.

This holds for two Jewish cities; how much more is it
incumbent upon a Jew who lives in a non-Jewish city, to
leave it and to move to a more propitious city. He should
try his utmost to do this, even if by so doing he endangers
himself; he should emigrate from a city in which he cannot
properly fulfill the law until he reaches one favorable to

his aims. For we find that Abraham, our father, peace be with him, rejected his family and his home, and emigrated in order to escape the spirit of those who deny God. Even if those who deny God do not force anyone to do as they do, we should still go forth from among them. But if they force a man to transgress one of the commandments, then he is forbidden to remain in that place. He must go forth, leave all that is his, journey day and night until he has found a place where he can carry out the law; the world is great and wide. To plead the consideration of one's house and one's family is, indeed, no extenuation: "No man can by any means redeem his brother, nor give to God a ransom for him." Whoever refers to such matters to ease his conscience, is worthless in my eyes. Rather should he emigrate to a worthy place, and in no case shall he remain in a place where faith is persecuted. He who remains in such a place must be deemed a sinner; he desecrates the name of God, and almost resembles one who sins deliberately.

From that day on when we were exiled from our land, we have been persecuted for our faith unceasingly. May God end these persecutions and make real his promise: "In those days, and in that time, saith the Lord, the iniquity of Israel shall be sought for, and there shall be none; and the sins of Judah, and they shall not be found: for I will pardon them whom I leave as a remnant." May this be his will. Amen.

EXPULSION FROM SPAIN

Isaac ben Judah Abrabanel

Portugal—Italy, 15th—16th Century

FROM HIS COMMENTARY ON THE EARLIER PROPHETS

Thus spake Isaac, the son of my lord, of the prince and great man in Israel, Judah Abrabanel, of the root of Jesse the Bethlehemite, of the seed of David, a leader and commander to my people, of a people scattered abroad and dispersed, one of those exiled from Jerusalem to Spain:

Behold, in expounding the books, that is to say, Joshua,
Judges, Samuel, and Kings, I encountered in reverse order
what Hiel the Bethelite encountered when he built up
Jericho, he who laid the foundation thereof with the loss
of his first-born, and with the loss of his youngest son he
set up the gates of it. But I opened my mouth to God in
former days that were better than these, settling on my
leas in the kingdom of Portugal, the land of my birth, to
expound those four books, since I saw that those who
had expounded them had done so inadequately. But with
the burden of the king and princes it came up upon my
neck, and I could not complete it until the hand of the
Lord touched me, and the king of Portugal held me for
his enemy, not for any injustice in my hands. He stood
with his right hand as an adversary to destroy me utterly;
he took all that was mine, durable and lawful possessions,
and I saved myself, I alone, fleeing to the kingdom of Castille from the oppressing sword. And when I arrived there,
a stranger in the land, a wayfaring man that turneth aside
to tarry for a night, I sought to repay that which God had
lent me by expounding the three first books, Joshua,
Judges, and Samuel.

All this happened at the beginning of the two hundred
and forty-fourth year, in the sixth millennium of the creation. And when I was about to begin expounding the Books
of the Kings, I was called to come in unto the king, to the
king of Spain, the greatest of all the kings on earth, who
ruled over the kingdoms of Castille, Aragon, Cataluñia,
and Sicily, and the other islands of the sea. I came to the
court of the king and the queen, was with them many days,
and the Lord gave me favor in their eyes, in the eyes of
the princes that sat first in the kingdom, and I wrought
in their service for eight years.

And both riches and honor, which if a man do, he lives
by them, I gained in their towns and in their castles. Therefore the Torah was slacked and the work hindered. Because I served the kings of peoples who are not of the
children of Israel, I left mine heritage, the kingdom of
Judah and of Israel, and the expounding of their books.

In the year two hundred and fifty-two, [1492] the king
of Spain conquered the entire kingdom of Granada and

the great city of Granada, great among nations and princess among the provinces, and in his might and pride he turned from his former ways. He imputed his might unto his God. "And Esau said in his heart": For wherewith could I reconcile myself unto my master, who has girded me with strength to battle, wherewith shall I come before the Lord, who has put this city into my hands, if not that I bring under his wings the people that walks in darkness, the scattered sheep of Israel, and either lead back to his law and his faith the backsliding daughter, or banish them from my countenance and cast them into another land, so that they may no longer dwell in my land nor tarry in my sight.

And because of this the king's commandment and his decree went forth, and a herald loudly proclaimed: "To you it is commanded, to all the families of the house of Israel, that if you 'go through the water,' [1] if you fall down and worship the gods of these peoples, you shall eat the good of the land, as we are doing this very day, and you shall dwell and trade therein. But if you refuse and rebel, if you do not mention the name of my God, and if you do not worship my God, rise up, and get you forth from among my people, out of the lands of Spain, Sicily, Mallorca, and Sardinia, which are under my rule, and three months after, there shall not a hoof be left behind of all who call themselves by the name of Jacob, or by the name of Israel, in any of the provinces of my kingdom."

Now since I was in the court of the king's house, I wore myself out with crying and my throat dried. Oftentimes I spoke to the king, I entreated him with my mouth, and said: "Help, O king, wherefore dealest thou thus with thy servants? Ask me ever so much dowry and gift, gold and silver and all that a man of the house of Israel has, will he give for his land."

I called for my lovers that see the king's face, to plead for my people. The nobles took counsel together, with all their might to implore the king to reverse the letters of his anger and fury, and to destroy the scheme he had devised against the Jews. But like the deaf adder he stopped his ear

----

[1] Allusion to baptismal water.

and answered nothing at all to anyone. And the queen stood at his right hand to accuse. With her much fair speech she caused him to yield, and bring to pass his act, to begin and also make an end. We labored but our fears were not mitigated. I was not at ease, neither was I quiet, neither had I rest; but trouble came.

And when the people heard these evil tidings, they mourned. And in every province whithersoever the king's commandment and his decree came, there was great mourning among the Jews. All trembled exceedingly, as with the anguish of her who bringeth forth her first child; there had been nothing like it since the day Judah was carried away out of his land, and into a strange land. And they said one to another: "Let us be of good courage, and let us prove strong for our law, and for the teachings of our God, before the voice of him that reproacheth and blasphemeth, the enemy and avenger. If they save us alive, we shall live; and if they kill us, we shall but die. But we will not break our covenant. Our heart shall not turn back, and we will walk in the name of the Lord our God."

And they went without strength, three hundred thousand on foot, the people among whom I am, young and old, little children and women, in one day, from all the provinces of the king. "Whither the spirit was to go, they went." "And their king passed before them and the Lord at the head of them." One said: " 'I am the Lord's,' and another subscribed with his hand unto the Lord." Some went to the kingdom of Portugal and to the kingdom of Navarra, which were near by, but behold, trouble and darkness pursued them; they were driven into darkness. Many evils and troubles befell them, wasting and destruction, famine and pestilence. Some made a way in the sea, and a path in the mighty waters. For indeed the hand of the Lord was against them to destroy them. For many of the children of the desolate were sold for bondmen and bondwomen in the districts of the nations, and many also "sank in the Red Sea . . . they sank as lead in the mighty waters." And there were such among them as went through fire and through water, for their ships were charred, and the fire of the Lord burned among them. And the conclusion of the whole matter was that his stern judgment omitted

none. Such as were for the sword, to the sword; and such
as were for the famine, to the famine; and such as were for
the captivity, to the captivity! The Lord made the pestilence cleave unto them, and they became an astonishment
and a byword among all nations, until they were utterly
consumed with terrors, and there were left but a few of
many, according to the words of our fathers: "Behold, we
perish, we are undone, we are all undone"; "Blessed be
the name of the Lord."

I too chose out their way, the way of a ship in the midst
of the sea. I, among the captives, came with all my house—
"the children are my children, and the flocks are my flocks"
—came here to Naples, to that exalted city, whose kings
are merciful kings, and I spoke with my own heart: I will
pay that which I have vowed, I will expound the Books
of the Kings, which I have not done until now; and I shall
do this also because "it is time to work for the Lord," to
commemorate the destruction of our holy and glorious
house, and the exile that has come upon our people, as
they are written in this book, and as I will expound with
the help of God.

Now, after all this: Hiel the Bethelite, in the building
of Jericho, had laid "the foundation thereof with his first-
born, and with his youngest son set up the gates thereof,"
but I, a man that hath seen affliction, began my explanation of these four books, and founded it upon the least of
the banishments and exiles that came upon me, that is,
the particular exile from the kingdom of Portugal, and
with the greatest of the exiles, the bitter and hasty exile,
the great and dreadful destruction, devoured and swal-
lowed, driven from abiding in Spain—with this I "set up
the gates" of this commentary and completed it.

THEY SHALL WANDER FROM
SEA TO SEA

Judah ben Jacob Hayyat

Spain—Italy, 15th–16th Century

FROM MINHAT YEHUDAH

And when I, Judah, the son of my wise, pious, and perfect master, Rabbi Jacob Hayyat, peace be upon him, was in Spain, I tasted a little of the sweet joy of learning, my eyes were filled with light, and I set my heart upon searching and delving into the realm of knowledge. I "went from strength to strength" in gathering all that now exists of the book I have mentioned. I gathered a little here and a little there until most of what now exists was in my hands. And I believe with absolute faith that the merit I thus acquired stood me in good stead throughout all the troubles that befell me in the course of the expulsion from Spain, troubles that will cause the ears of all who hear them to ring. I do not know how to recount all these troubles in full, but I shall relate some of them and shall speak the praises of the Lord.

My family and I, together with two hundred and fifty other souls, sailed in one small boat from the great city of Lisbon in the kingdom of Portugal, in midwinter, at the command of the king, in the year 1493. And the Lord, blessed be he, smote us with the pestilence to fulfill the words of Scripture: "I shall smite them with the pestilence and destroy them." That was the reason why there was no place where anyone would receive us. "Be off with you, unclean ones," was their cry unto us. And so we sailed the sea, wandering and tossing about, for four months, with but little bread and scant water. At the end of this time a Biscay boat came upon us. We were taken captive, deprived of our wealth, and brought to the great city of Malaga in Spain. There we lay at anchor against our wishes, for we were permitted neither to go ashore nor to sail from there. Each day priests would come aboard our ship at the order of the bishop, to hold sermons before us.

They kept repeating to us: "Return, return, O Shulammite; return, return, that we may look upon thee." And we
would answer: "What will ye see in the Shulammite? As it
were a dance of two companies."

And when they realized the devotion and the tenacity
with which we clung to our God, the bishop placed an
interdict upon them that they give us no bread, and no
water, and no provisions whatsoever. Perhaps that would
cause us to seek conversion. This went on for five days,
and throughout those days the rulers and grandees of the
city, in the company of learned priests, kept coming aboard
our ship and saying to us: "How long will you refuse to
hearken unto us?"— referring to the verse: "Who is the man
that desireth life?" Thereupon close to one hundred souls
apostatized in one day, since they could not withstand this
bitter trial, and since those who died by the sword were
more fortunate than those who died by starvation. Those
of us who remained—a few out of many—were strengthened
in our resolve to prefer death, for we said: "It is better
that we die at the hand of the Lord."

Then my dear innocent wife, peace be unto her, expired
of hunger and thirst; also, maidens and young men, the
old and the young, altogether close to fifty souls. As for me
too there was but a step between me and death. There was
then indeed fulfilled that which the prophet, peace be
upon him, had foretold: "And they shall wander from
sea to sea, and from the north even to the east. . . . In
that day shall the fair virgins and the young men faint for
thirst." "Out of our straits we called upon the Lord; he
answered us with great enlargement." And out of affliction
respite did come, for the bishop revoked the interdict, once
he saw how stubbornly we clung to our God. From then on
we were brought all kinds of food, and we lay there at
anchor another two months, against our wishes, until we
were finally permitted to go at will. From there we set sail
for the Barbary coast, in the kingdom of Fez.

In the Moslem country the people are evil and great
sinners against the Lord. What the pestilence left behind,
the locust consumed. There too I found neither peace nor
rest. A certain Moslem who had come from Spain lived in
the same house with me. He happened to be there because

his people too had been subjected to expulsion. He brought charges against me that when I was in Spain, I had ordered the Jews of my community, among whom I served as teacher of the Law, to make an effigy of Mohammed, the prophet of the Moslems, and to drag it again and again through the market places and streets of the city at a time when the holy congregations were holding joyous celebrations over the conquest of the great city of Granada [by the Christians]. His charges were given credence upon the alleged testimony of three witnesses. Thereupon I was beaten and wounded. I was stripped of my clothes, cast into a pit full of snakes and scorpions, and soon thereafter condemned to be stoned to death. They assured me, however, that if I would apostatize, I would be set up as prince and ruler over them, not to mention the reward and gifts I would receive. But the Lord in whom I placed my trust confounded their evil devices, although I stayed there close to forty days in pitch darkness, with sparing bread and scant water, and my stomach sagged to the ground from hunger and thirst, and I was naked and lacking everything. And the Lord stirred the spirit of the Jews of Susa and they came to ransom us. I gave them almost two hundred books that I had, in return for the ransom they paid.

After I left there I proceeded to the great city of Fez. Famine prevailed in this city, until we were reduced to eating the grass in the fields. Every day I ground grain with my two hands at the homes of the Moslems, in return for a small slice of bread, thinner than thin, not fit even for dogs to eat. And during the nights my stomach sagged to the ground and my swollen belly was my bolster. Because of the intense autumn cold, because we had no covering against the cold, and also because we had no houses in which to spend the night, we used to dig holes in the rubbish heaps in the city and burrow into them. Then were fulfilled the words: "They who were brought up in scarlet embrace dunghills." And then I managed to get to the kingdom of Naples, after much wandering and troubles too numerous to count. But even there I found neither peace, nor quiet, nor rest, for trouble came, ushered in by the king of France. I was included in the general roundup of all the Jews of the kingdom, and again I was beaten, and wounded, and stripped of all my clothes and of all that I had.

After that, I came, clothed in rags, to the great city of Venice, by way of the sea. When the Spanish grandees who were there saw me, their eyes brimmed with tears and they clad me. May the Lord requite their work and may the Lord succor them in the day of evil.

If my strength was the strength of stone, if my flesh was of brass to withstand all these misfortunes, it was no doubt by merit of my efforts and my exertions in pursuit of knowledge, which stood by me and strengthened me measure for measure, just as I took hold of her when there was none to uphold her.

From the city of Venice I made my way to the great city of Mantua. There I found a certain scholar from Spain, Rabbi Joseph Jabez, a survivor of the expulsion, a man righteous in all his ways and gracious in all his works, as fine in his practice as he was in his preachings. He, along with other wise and important personages, requested of me that I prepare a commentary to the *Order of God,* since they were eager to behold the graciousness of the Lord and to visit early in his temple. I was inclined to fulfill their desire and withheld nothing from them.

THE DEATH OF THE MARTYRS

Abraham ben Eliezer ha-Levi

Spain, 15th–16th Century

FROM MEGILLAT AMRAPHEL

This is a tradition among the sages: If someone resolves in his heart to sacrifice himself for the honor of His great name—come what will, and come what may—such a man will not feel the torment of wounds, which torment only those who are not resolved with their whole heart. Now, if one leads such a man forth, in order to subject him to the pain and agony of terrible torture—as it came to pass with the holy martyrs, the bloom of youth, the sons of Hannah, the martyr, in the days of the Maccabees, those who were standing before God, the heroes who fought God's battles and if, in that hour, such a man directs all his powers toward gazing at the mighty name of God, which is written in the space between his eyes, and resolves in his heart to sanctify him; and if his eyes gaze upon the Holy One of Israel, and if he concentrates his heart and his mind upon him with all the strength he is capable of, so that the holy name turns into burning fire, and the letters in it shine over the fullness of the world; or if he can make the letters grow as much as it is in his power: then indeed can he be certain in his heart that he will resist temptation. His mind is firm, it is secure in God. He will not feel the pain of wounds and torture, and it will not be possible to make him tremble with the fear of death. And though this may seem improbable to human reason, it has been experienced and related by the sages and the holy martyrs.

But concerning the manner in which he shall resolve to sanctify His name, when they torture him, and examine him, and probe him, and promise to release him and to stop torturing him if he will consent to deny honor to God, or if they request him to say what he desires to be—concerning this I found that a devout man wrote:

This shall be your answer: "What do you want of me? Yes, I am a Jew. As a Jew will I live, and as a Jew will I die —as a Jew, a Jew, a Jew!" And then he shall resolve in his heart what his lips have shaped and his mouth has spoken, and he shall be steadfast and of firm purpose to sanctify his Creator, and not to desecrate the name of God. Then he will be impervious to torture. And the prophet Isaiah was referring to this mystery when he said: "One shall say: 'I am the Lord's'; and another shall call himself by the name of Jacob; and another shall subscribe with his hand unto the Lord, and surname himself by the name of Israel." And these words are worthy to be spread abroad in Israel, for this era is an era of persecution, and it is a good thing that the principle of the sanctification of the name should be familiar to everyone who is named after Israel. For who knows, who knows what the day will bring, and what will be the end of man!

But concerning the soul of the martyr who delivers his soul up to God and his body to the pyre, who persists in love for him, and dies in the midst of the wicked—concerning that, Solomon said: "Who is this that cometh up from the wilderness, shattered for the sake of her beloved?" For God's word is clear: she is shattered, and falls limb for limb, piece for piece. And the righteous who dwell in the innermost reaches of the king's palace, where joy has her habitation, say of the soul of the martyr: Who is that coming up from the lower world, which is like a wilderness where there are nothing but serpents and adders, scorpions and thirst? For the love of her friend, her body falls to pieces in the terrible judgment wreaked upon it. They grip her flesh with tongs heated to a white glow, or they hack it to pieces with the sword. But God, the Lord of peace, for love of whom she has suffered all this, looks down from the place of his dwelling and says of the martyr whose soul is rising up to him: Behold, you are clean and straight. Today have I born you anew, and "awakened thee under the apple tree," in the orchards of paradise. Your soul, which has suffered martyrdom, is purified, and "comes before her mother," the throne of my glory, whence it broke forth. For where the throne is, the mother of all souls, "there thy mother was in travail with thee, there was she in travail and brought thee forth."

And the martyr answers his Creator in the words of the Song of Songs: "Set me as a seal upon thy heart, as a seal upon thine arm," and do not forget me in all eternity. Remember the love with which I loved you, for even if they kill me because of my love for you, I shall not feel it, "for love is strong as death." Even if they buried me alive, all this would be nothing to me, for my "zeal is cruel as the grave," my zeal for the honor of your name. And if they burn me and cast me into the fire, this too is nothing compared to my love of you, for my love of you is a miracle that has been wrought upon me, and burns within me like torches, "the flashes thereof are flashes of fire, a very flame of the Lord." How, then, could my soul suffer from that little fire, while the leaping flame of love for you swells and burns within me! Disaster and torture, which are like water, cannot quench the fires of my love. And though my persecutors come upon me like a flood, my spirit drives me to yield myself up for you. I am not speaking of my wealth, for wealth is less than nothing, and if anyone were to boast that he gave "all the substance of his house for love," those who are perfected, those who come before God, would scorn him, for it is nothing to them, and they hold the treasures of the world in contempt. But there is something a man may boast of—that he surrenders his body to the pyre and to all those other terrible tortures I spoke of, for this is valid before God, and he sets him as a seal upon his arm, and twines him around his heart like a string of jewels. His soul shines in God's light, and there is no eye that has seen the bliss that awaits him. For his station and his power are great, and his place is among those who are "pitched on the east side toward the rising of the sun," with Moses and Aaron, among those who were slain by Rome, and those who were slain in Lud. He is worth a whole world, and his works praise him in the gates.

A JEW I SHALL REMAIN

Solomon ibn Verga

Spain—Italy, 15th–16th Century

FROM THE SHEBET YEHUDAH

I heard from some of the elders who came out of Spain that one of the boats was infested with the plague, and the captain of the boat put the passengers ashore at some uninhabited place. And there most of them died of starvation, while some of them gathered up all their strength to set out on foot in search of some settlement.

There was one Jew among them who struggled on afoot together with his wife and two children. The wife grew faint and died, because she was not accustomed to so much difficult walking. The husband carried his children along until both he and they fainted from hunger. When he regained consciousness, he found that his two children had died.

In great grief he rose to his feet and said: "O Lord of all the universe, you are doing a great deal that I might even desert my faith. But know you of a certainty that—even against the will of heaven—a Jew I am and a Jew I shall remain. And neither that which you have brought upon me nor that which you will yet bring upon me will be of any avail."

Thereupon he gathered some earth and some grass, and covered the boys, and went forth in search of a settlement.

THE SUPREME SACRIFICE

Alexander Süsskind

Lithuania, 18th Century

FROM HIS TESTAMENT

Besides the potential surrender of life that every Israelite is bound to take upon himself when reciting the Shma and certain prayers, as I have indicated in my treatise in accordance with the views of the Zohar and of Isaac Luria—besides this, I command you, my beloved children, that if you be called upon to suffer actual martyrdom (from which God deliver you and all the holy people!), you shall go to your death with wholehearted joy. And the Creator will delight in you throughout the realms above. He will say: "See what manner of man I made in my world; he spared not his body, but bore chastisements for my honor, and delivered himself up for the sanctification of my name!" And my heart knows that if I were myself required to make this supreme sacrifice, it would not be for the wondrous reward that eye has not seen in the worlds on high, but solely for the great name of God, that it might be magnified and sanctified in all worlds below and above, by my act of voluntary martyrdom.

THE HOLY LAND

THE HOLY LAND OF ISRAEL

Nahman of Bratzlav

Ukraine, 18th–19th Century

All the holiness of Israel clings to Erez Israel, and every
time a man cleanses and purifies his soul, he conquers and
liberates a portion of the land. The demons rage: "You
are robbers who have conquered a land that was not
yours!" That is why a man should not spend all his effort
upon the Torah, but some also upon the world, and draw
love down upon everything, so that the accusation will be
invalid, and all will come and join and yield themselves
up to holiness.

Erez Israel and the Torah are one and the same thing.
And had the land not previously been in the hands of the
Canaanites, it would have spewed out Israel, those who
sinned against the Torah, and never would they have been
allowed to return. That was why the sheath had to be in
existence before the core of the fruit, and the land had to
remain in the hands of the Canaanites, for many years.
But in reality, it was holy even then, for holiness was innate
in it from time immemorial, save that then it was well
hidden and none knew of it until our father Abraham
came and began to reveal the holiness of the land. For he
was a man of love. Love that seeks no returns was the
quality with which he sustained the world before the

Torah was given, and it was this very love that was hidden in Erez Israel: it was the hidden Torah, for Erez Israel and the Torah are one and the same thing. Then, when Israel received the Torah, and came to Erez Israel, they were able to continue in the revelation of holiness, and to lift hidden holiness into the open. And so, even though later on they offended the holiness that had been made apparent, and were lacking in the fulfillment of the Torah, they could still long endure in Erez Israel, because of the strength of that love which seeks no returns, and that hidden Torah. And even now that we are exiled from our land for the vast number of our transgressions, Erez Israel still persists in holiness because of the strength of the hidden Torah and the love that seeks no returns, the love that was hidden in the land even when it was still in the hands of the Canaanites. That is why we are always waiting to return to our land, for we know that in secret it is ours.

THE SACRED PLACE

Judah ha-Levi

Spain—Palestine, 11th–12th Century

FROM THE KUZARI

The master was then anxious to leave the land of Chazar and betake himself to Jerusalem. The king was reluctant to have him go and expressed his feeling in these words: What is it that you seek in Jerusalem and the land of Canaan, now that the Divine Presence is no longer there? If one's desire is great and one's mind pure, it is possible to approach God in any place. Why face dangers on land and water and among various peoples?

The master answered: The visible Presence has, indeed, disappeared, because it does not reveal itself save to a prophet, or in a favored community, or in a place set apart. This is what we look for in the passage, "For they shall see, eye to eye, the Lord returning to Zion," and what we say

in our prayers: "Let our eyes behold when Thou re-
turnest to Zion." As regards the invisible and spiritual
Presence, it is with every born Israelite who leads a virtuous
life, who has a pure heart and an upright mind before the
God of Israel. The land of Canaan is in special favor with
the God of Israel, and no function can be perfect except
there. Heart and soul are wholly pure and immaculate
only in the place believed to be specially selected by God.
If this is true in a figurative sense, how much more so in
reality! So the longing for this springs from disinterested
motives, particularly for him who wishes to live there and
atone for past transgressions, since he has had no opportunity to offer the sacrifices ordained by God for intentional
and unintentional sins. He is supported by the saying of
the sages, "Wandering atones for sins," [1] especially if his
wandering brings him to the place of God's choice. The
dangers he runs on land and on sea do not belong to the
category of "You shall not tempt the Lord," for this verse
refers to risks one takes when traveling with merchandise
in the hope of gain. He who incurs even greater dangers
because of his ardent desire to obtain forgiveness, is free
from reproach if he has balanced the account of his years,
expressed gratitude for his past life, and exults in spending
the remainder of his days in seeking the favor of the Lord.
He braves danger and gives fervent praise to God if he
escapes. But should he perish through his sins, he has ob-
tained the divine favor, and may be confident of having
atoned for most of his sins by his death. In my opinion
this is better than to seek the dangers of war in order to
win fame and gain spoils through courage and endurance.
This kind of danger is inferior even to that of men who go
to war for hire.

The Chazar king said: I thought you loved freedom,
yet now you seem willing to assume new religious duties,
which you will be obliged to fulfill in the Land of Israel
but which are in abeyance here.

The master said: I seek freedom only from serving the
many people whose favor means nothing to me, and which
I should never gain though I worked for it all my life. And
even if I could obtain it, serving men and courting their

1 Sanhedrin 37 b.

favor still would not profit me. I prefer to seek the service
of One whose favor is gained by even a small effort, and
yet helps in this world and in the coming world. This is
the favor of God. To serve him is true freedom; to be
humble before him, true honor. . . . It is written: "Thou
wilt arise, and have compassion upon Zion; for it is time
to be gracious unto her, for the appointed time is come.
For Thy servants take pleasure in her stones, and love
her dust." This means that Jerusalem can be rebuilt only
when Israel will yearn for this so deeply that they love
her stones and her dust.

The Chazar king said: If this be so, it would be a sin
to hinder you. Rather is it a merit to assist you. May God
grant you his help and be your protector and friend. May
he favor you in his mercy.

WITHIN THE GATES OF DESOLATE JERUSALEM

Moses Nahmanides

Spain—Palestine, 13th Century

FROM HIS COMMENTARY ON THE PENTATEUCH

"Our feet are standing within thy gates, O Jerusalem,"
house of the Lord and gate of heaven. "Jerusalem that art
builded as a city that is compact together" with the one in
heaven built. "Whither the tribes went up, even the tribes
of the Lord," where is the foundation stone from which
the world was started, whence are woven the foundations
of the universe and their boundary, and where is Mount
Moriah from which go forth Torah and wisdom—the
mount which the Lord desired for his abode and upon
which he built his house of repose.

And the fruit of the land is a source of pride and glory.
Its fruits and crops are plentiful and it still flows with milk
and honey for those who dwell in it. I liken you, my
motherland, unto a woman whose newborn child has died

at her bosom, and the milk in her breasts gives her but
pain and she gives suck to the young of dogs.

"I am the man that hath seen affliction": I have wandered far from my household, left friend and acquaintance
far behind, for my journey has stretched far, far afield. I
have become a recluse among my brethren, my home the
wayfarer's desert resting place. I have left my home, abandoned my inheritance, and there have I left my spirit and
my soul behind, with my sons and daughters, who are as
my own soul, and with the children whom I have brought
up and dandled on my knees. They are my beloved, my
fond ones. And my hopes and heart were there all the
days. . . . Yet it is easy to spurn this and all the glory
my eyes have seen. Better is it in my eyes to spend but a
day in Your court, to visit early in Your destroyed temples,
and to gaze upon Your desolate sanctuary. . . .

THE LAND IS BLESSED

Moses Nahmanides

Spain—Palestine, 13th Century

A LETTER FROM JERUSALEM

The blessings of the Lord be upon you, my son Nahman!
O that you might behold Jerusalem happy, and the children of your children! May your board be like that of our
ancestor Abraham! I am writing this letter in the holy city
of Jerusalem. Thanks to Him, the keeper of my weal, I
was fortunate enough to arrive here safe and sound, on
the ninth day of the month of Elul, and stayed until the
day after Yom Kippur. Now I plan to go to Hebron, the
burial place of our fathers, there to prostrate myself and
carve out my grave.

What shall I tell you about this country? It is barren
and abandoned. To describe it briefly: the holier the
places, the more waste! Jerusalem suffered worse destruction than all the other towns, the land of Judea more than

Galilee. But in spite of this destruction, the land is still
blessed. It has about two thousand inhabitants, among
them three hundred Christians who escaped the sultan's
sword. There are not many Jews, for they fled at the coming of the Tartars, and some fell by the sword. Two
brothers live there, dyers by trade, who buy their dyes
from the sovereign. The people come to their house to
pray, and on the Sabbath hold the service there. But we
urged them on, and succeeded in finding an empty house
that is built on marble columns and has a beautiful vaulted
roof. We took this for our synagogue. For the property
in this city is unowned, and whoever wants to take possession of a deserted house, may do so. We all contributed
to the furnishing of the house and sent to Sichem for a
few Torah scrolls that had been sent there for safekeeping
when the Tartars invaded Jerusalem. The synagogue will
soon be ready, and regular services will be held in it. For
people are always coming to Jerusalem, men and women
from Damascus, Aleppo, and all parts of the country, to
see the site of the Temple and to lament. May He who
constrained to us to see Jerusalem destroyed, also grant
us the joy of seeing it rebuilt and restored when the glory
of his Presence returns there.

But you, my son, and your brothers and kinsmen, may
you all be found worthy of seeing the joy of Jerusalem and
the solace of Zion! Your father Moses ben Nahman, blessed
be the memory of the righteous!

THE AGREEMENT

Jacob ben Hananel and Hiskiah

Spain, 13th–14th Century

FROM A LETTER TO ASHER BEN YEHIEL

For the honor of the God of Israel, who elected Jerusalem
as his settled place to abide in forever, and for the honor
of his perfect Torah, which proceeds from Zion, "for there

the Lord commanded the blessing, even life for ever," we have assumed certain obligations, we who have signed below. We have vowed unto the mighty God of Jacob to go into the Land of Israel, into the land of the living, to dwell in Jerusalem or near unto it, as we shall decide, to do the will of God and to serve him with our whole hearts, for there man can fulfill the commandments, and take upon himself the kingdom of heaven, and perform acceptable service, because there is the house of our God and the gate of heaven.

So we both took an oath. One swore to the other upon the scroll of the Torah, according to the divine will, that we would be friends to each other for seven years from the day on which we leave this country: one was not to break friendship with the other during that time. And if it be the will of the Creator that we find a way to earn a livelihood for ourselves and the people of our house, then we both shall set a time aside for the Torah. If, however, God forbid, sin should bring about that we do not both find work to provide a livelihood, then one of us shall set aside time for studying the Torah, for a certain span, while his friend occupies himself with worldly matters, so that— through either labor, or trading, or teaching—he may provide for him who has given himself up to learning the Torah, and for the people of both their houses. If it is possible for him, then he too shall set aside time for studying the Torah. But if, after a certain period, he who is laboring in the affairs of this world wishes to devote himself to the study of the Torah, then his friend shall work to provide for their wives and the people of their houses, just as the other has been doing; and so on, each in turn. And all the earnings that the Creator accords shall be for us both, to provide for us and the people of our houses— for each according to his needs, according to what is due him and the people of his house—both for those who are there today and for those who will be born to him from today on, in time to come, but not for those who may join him because they so desire. If, however, God forbid, the labors of the one do not suffice to provide for both houses, then shall both of us work in the affairs of this world, so that we may keep alive our souls and the souls of those who belong to our houses. And all that we earn, the one more, the one less, shall be in common between us, nor shall one of us say: "I earn more, and wish to provide for myself more lavishly, according to my earnings." No, we must both share equally in all that we earn. And from that hour on in which we leave to travel on the road from Cordoba, we shall remain together and be partners in all earnings the Creator accords, no matter how we earn— whether through work or otherwise. If, however, God forbid, something should befall one of us, and make it impossible for him to go up into the Land of Israel, then his friend shall not be bound by his vow or by his oath, until the other is again able to fulfill it. For only on this condition did we take upon ourselves the vow and the oath— that during all the time that we are together as friends, the vow shall be a vow, and the oath an oath; but if this is not so, then the vow shall no longer be a vow, nor the oath an oath.

THE STRENGTH OF WANTING

Isaac Luria

Palestine, 16th Century

FROM THE SHIBHEI HA-ARI

Once, on the eve of the Sabbath, just before "the bride Sabbath was brought in," the master went forth from the city of Safed with his disciples. He wore four white garments, the upper cloak, the caftan, the coat, and the trousers, thus to receive the Sabbath. He began chanting the psalm, "Ascribe unto the Lord, O ye sons of might," and the song that ushers in the Sabbath, and the "Psalm for the Sabbath day," and "The Lord reigneth," each with its own beautiful melody.

And in the middle of his singing, he spoke to his disciples and said: "My friends, do you want to go to Jerusalem before the Sabbath, so that we may celebrate it in Jerusalem?"

But Jerusalem is more than twenty-five parasangs away from Safed.

Then some of the disciples replied, "We want to do this," but others answered, saying, "Let us first go home and tell our wives about it."

When they said, "Let us go home first," the master shook with a mighty tremor, struck his hands together, and said: "Woe to us that we were not worthy to be redeemed. Had you all answered me, as though with one voice, and in great gladness, that you wanted to go, of a sudden all Israel would have been redeemed. For the hour of redemption was at hand. But when you hesitated, exile again became what it has been, because of our great failings."

IN JERUSALEM

Obadiah of Bertinoro

Italy—Palestine, 15th–16th Century

FROM HIS LETTERS ON A JOURNEY

It is about three miles from Bethlehem to Jerusalem. Vineyards and olive groves line the entire way. On this stretch the vineyards are like those in the region of Romagna, for the vines grow short and thick. Approximately three fourths of a mile from Jerusalem, from the place where you begin to go downhill by a path descending in terraces, we saw the holy city, the citadel of our delight. There we rent our garments, in accordance with the law. And after a little time we saw the broken house of our sanctuary and glory, and we rent our garments a second time for the sake of the sanctuary. Thus we reached the gates of Jerusalem, and entered the city on the thirteenth day of the month of Nisan, in the year 5248 [1488]. At noon of this day "our feet stood within thy gates, O Jerusalem."

There an Ashkenazic Jew who had grown up in Italy came to meet me. He took me to his house, and during all the days of Passover I remained there as his guest.

Most of Jerusalem is in ruins and deserted, and it goes without saying that there is no wall around the city. The people in it—so I am told—are about four thousand heads of families in number; only seventy heads of families are Jews. No more than these are left; they are poor people and have no possessions. There is hardly one who has enough bread. Whoever has bread for a year is called rich in this place, at the time I am writing. There are many widows, old and young, Ashkenazic and Sephardic folk and also such as speak other tongues—seven women to every man.

Here the Jews certainly do not suffer hardship from the Ismaelites. I walked through the whole length and breadth of the land, and there was none "that opened the mouth or chirped." They are very charitable to strangers, and especially to such as do not know their language. And even when they see many Jews together, they do not envy them. And according to my estimation, if there were a man here wise and versed in governing a country, he could be an elder and a judge for the Ismaelites as well as for the Jews. But among all the Jews in these regions, there is none who would be agreeable to men.

Today I found myself lodgings in Jerusalem. I live near the house of prayer; my bedroom is upstairs, close to the wall of the house of prayer. Five persons inhabit the court whe. e I have my lodging: they are all women, no man save one who is blind, whose wife tends to my wants when I require it. And it is for me to give thanks to God that he has blessed me all the way here, that I have not fallen ill, like the rest of the folk who came with me. For most people who come to Jerusalem from a distant country fall ill, and are confined to bed, because of the change of air and the rapid change from heat to cold, and cold to heat, from one moment to the next. All the winds in the world come and blow in Jerusalem. They say that every wind comes and prostrates itself unto God in Jerusalem, before going to that place to which it wants to go. Blessed be he who knows the truth!

Today I am living in the house of our illustrious lord, who has set me above his house here in Jerusalem. Twice this month, I expounded to the congregation in the house of prayer. I used the holy tongue, which most of them understand. And so I am to them "as a love song of one that hath a pleasant voice, and can play well on an instrument." When I expound, they praise and exalt me, and hear my words—"but they do them not."

ZION FORGOTTEN

Jacob Emden

Germany, 18th Century

FROM THE INTRODUCTION OF HIS PRAYER BOOK

Everyone in Israel must in his heart steadfastly resolve to go to Erez Israel and to remain there. But if he cannot go himself, he should, if his circumstances permit—whether he be a craftsman or a merchant—support some person in that country, and so do his part in restoring the Holy Land, which has been laid waste, by maintaining one of its rightful inhabitants.

He must feel the desire to pray there before the King's palace, to which the Divine Presence still clings, even in its destruction. Therefore he who does not live in that country cannot give perfect service to God.

You shall not plan—God forbid—to settle in a place not in that country. The mistake our parents made was that of ignoring this precious land, and thereby they caused much suffering in the generations that came after them. The thought of this land was our solace in our bitter exile, when not one alone rose against us, for never could we find peace and rest. But when we forgot our yearning for that land, we ourselves were forgotten like the dead. Not

one in a thousand fared forth to settle there, perhaps only
one from a whole country, and two out of a whole generation. No heart longed for its love or was concerned with
its welfare, and no one yearned to behold it. Whenever
we found a little rest, we thought we had come upon a
new Land of Israel and a new Jerusalem. And misfortune
befell us because Israel lived in peace and enjoyed honors
in Spain and in other countries, for more than a thousand
years after the destruction of the Temple, and no son of
Israel remained in the Holy Land. God is just. They were
no longer aware that exile is their lot, and they mixed
with the people among whom they lived, and learned their
ways. No one at all yearned for Zion; it was abandoned
and forgotten. We did not think of returning to our home.
The city that contained the graves of our fathers was not
our goal. We shared the joys of others.

We asked: "Who is the wise man that he may understand this? Wherefore is the land perished and laid waste
like a wilderness? And the Lord saith: Because they have
forsaken My law." For Israel is called God's heritage, and
the land is his heritage, and the Torah is connected with
both, with the people of God and the heritage of God, and
whoever leaves the one has also abandoned the other.

HOW TO ENTER THE HOLY LAND

Abraham Kalisker

Poland—Palestine, 18th Century

A LETTER FROM TIBERIAS, CA. 1790

I think it is fitting to answer those who address inquiries
to me because they wish to live in the Holy Land. For this
it is necessary to know, and to give information, as to what
this land is really like.

Concerning the words, "Lord, Thou hast been favorable
unto Thy land," our teachers have said: God changes it

again and again, and regards it, and rests his eyes upon it, until it makes its deeds pleasing to him.[1]

Many, many changes and events, experiences, and fates befall every single man who comes to this land, until he adjusts to it, has joy in its stones, and loves its dust, until the ruins in the Land of Israel are dearer to him than a palace abroad, and dry bread in that place dearer than all delicacies elsewhere. But this does not happen in one day nor in two, not in a month, and not in a year. Many a year passes before the days of his initiation are over, his initiation into the true life. But then he lives in his native land, and always before God, as it is written, "But of Zion it shall be said: 'This man and that was born in her,' " which means that everyone who desires to go to the sanctuary requires a new conception and infancy, a new childhood, youth, etc., until he beholds the land face to face, until his soul is bound up with that of the land.

And that is how it is. He who comes and brings with him his knowledge, each what he has attained according to his degree, does not adjust in the beginning. His mind is bewildered, he is cast hither and yon without finding repose or security; he climbs up to very heaven and sinks into abysses, like a ship that is tossed about on the seas, and he troubles others with his concerns and actions. And of his mode of life in regard to the Torah and the commandments, this holds: What was, is no more—until God shows him the face of the land, and then he will arrive at rest and peace. But this is something that cannot be definitely gauged: the length of time, how, how much, and when—in each individual, all these matters depend on his affairs and actions and the root of his soul. Therefore let everyone who, with all his being, wishes to enter the Holy Land, consider all these things, and examine himself as to whether he has the strength to surmount everything, lest he lose even what he has had up to this time.

[1] Midrash Tehillim, on Ps. 85:1.

THE KINGDOM OF GOD

BEFORE THE GATES OF ROME

from the Talmud

Rabbi Joshua came upon the prophet Elijah as he was standing at the entrance of Rabbi Simeon ben Yohai's cave.

He asked him: "When is the Messiah coming?"

The other replied: "Go and ask him yourself."

"Where shall I find him?"

"Before the gates of Rome."

"By what sign shall I know him?"

"He is sitting among poor people covered with wounds. The others unbind all their wounds at once, and then bind them up again. But he unbinds one wound at a time, and binds it up again straightway. He tells himself: 'Perhaps I shall be needed [1]—and I must not take time and be late!' "

So he went and found him and said: "Peace be with you, my master and teacher!"

He answered him: "Peace be with you, son of Levi!"

Then he asked him: "When are you coming, master?"

He answered him: "Today!"

Thereupon he returned to Elijah and said to him: "He has deceived me, he has indeed deceived me! He told me, 'Today I am coming!' and he has not come.

But the other said to him: "This is what he told you: 'Today—if ye would but hearken to His voice.' "

[1] To appear as the Messiah.

THE SUFFERING SERVANT

from the Zohar

Spain, 13th Century

In the Garden of Eden there is a hall that is called the "hall of the afflicted." Now it is into this hall that the Messiah goes and summons all the afflictions and pains and sufferings of Israel to come upon him. And so they all come upon him. And had he not eased the children of Israel of their sorrow, and taken their burden upon himself, there would be none who could endure the suffering of Israel in penalty for neglecting the Torah. Thus it is written: "Surely our diseases he did bear and our pains he carried." As long as the children of Israel dwelt in the Holy Land, they averted all afflictions and sufferings from the world by the service of the sanctuary and by sacrifice. But now it is the Messiah who is averting them from the habitants of the world.

MESSIAH, THE ANOINTED KING

Moses Maimonides

Spain—Egypt, 12th Century

FROM THE MISHNEH TORAH

The Anointed King will in time arise and establish the kingdom of David in its former position and in the dominion it originally had. He will build up the sanctuary and gather the scattered of Israel. In his day, the laws will become what they were in olden times. They will bring offerings, they will make years of release and years of jubilee, according to the commandment given in the Torah.[1]

[1] Cf. Deut. 15:1–4; Lev. 25:8–24.

Whoever has no faith in him, or does not await his coming, rejects not only the other prophets, but also the Torah, and Moses, our master, for the Torah testifies to him, as it is written: "The Lord thy God will turn thy captivity, and have compassion upon thee, and will return and gather thee from all the peoples, whither the Lord thy God hath scattered thee. If any of thine that are dispersed be in the uttermost parts of heaven, from thence will the Lord thy God gather thee, and from thence will He fetch thee. And the Lord thy God will bring thee into the land which thy fathers possessed, and thou shalt possess it."

Do not think, however, that the Anointed King must give signs and miracles and create new things in this world, or bring the dead back to life, and the like. It will not be so. For see: Rabbi Akiba, who was a great sage among the sages of the Mishnah, it was he who carried arms for ben Koziba,[1] the king, and it was he who said of him that he was the Anointed King. He and all the sages of his generation thought that this was the Anointed King, until he was slain in his guilt. And after he was slain they all knew that he was not the Anointed King. But never had the sages asked him for a sign or for miracles. The root of these things is the following: This Torah, its statutes and its laws, are for all times. There is nothing one could add to it, and nothing one could take away.

If a king should arise out of the house of David, one who meditates upon the Torah, and like his ancestor, David, occupies himself with the commandments according to the written and the oral law, who has bent Israel to go in the ways of the Torah and to restore its breach, and who has fought the battles of the Lord, then it might be presumed that he is the Anointed. If he has succeeded, if he has built up the sanctuary in its place, if he has gathered the scattered of Israel, behold, then he is surely the Anointed. He will order the whole world, so that all together may serve the Lord, as it is written: "For then will I turn to the peoples a pure language, that they may all

[1] Ben Koziba ("Son of Lies") and Bar Kokba ("Son of the Star"): names applied to the leader of the Jewish revolt against the Romans in 132 C.E.

call upon the name of the Lord, to serve Him with one consent."

Do not think in your heart that in the days of the Anointed something will be changed in the ways of the world, or that an innovation will appear in the work of creation. No! The world will go its ways as before, and that which is said in Isaiah, "And the wolf shall dwell with the lamb, and the leopard shall lie down with the kid," is but a parable, and its meaning is that Israel will dwell in safety with the wicked among the heathen, and all will turn to the true faith; they will not rob nor destroy, and they will eat only what is permitted, in peace, like Israel, as it is written: "The lion shall eat straw like the ox." And everything else like this that is said concerning the Anointed, is also a parable. In the days of the Anointed all will know what the parable signified and what it was meant to imply.

The sages said: "Nothing, save the cessation of the servitude to the nations, distinguishes the days of the Anointed from our time." [1] From the words of the prophets, we see that in the early days of the Anointed a battle will take place "against Gog and Magog," and that before this battle against Gog and Magog, a prophet will arise who will make straight the people of Israel and prepare their hearts, as it is written: "Behold, I will send you Elijah the prophet before the coming of the great and terrible day of the Lord." But he comes only to bring peace into the world, as it is written: "And he shall turn the heart of the fathers to the children."

Among the sages there are some who say Elijah will come before the Anointed. But concerning these things and others of the same kind, none knows how they will be until they occur. For the prophets veil these things, and the sages have no tradition concerning them, save what they have deduced from the Scriptures, and so herein their opinion is divided. At any rate, neither the order of this event nor its details are the root of faith. A man must never ponder over legendary accounts, nor dwell upon interpretations

1 Sanhedrin 91 b.

dealing with them or with matters like them. He must not make them of primary importance, for they do not guide him either to fear or to love God. Nor may he seek to calculate the end. The sages said: "Let the spirit of those breathe its last, who seek to calculate the end." [1] Rather let him wait and trust in the matter as a whole, as we have expounded.

The sages and the prophets did not yearn for the days of the Anointed in order to seize upon the world, and not in order to rule over the heathen, or to be exalted by the peoples, or to eat and drink and rejoice, but to be free for the Torah and the wisdom within it, free from any goading and intrusion, so that they may be worthy of life in the coming world.

When that time is here, none will go hungry, there will be no war, no zealousness, and no conflict, for goodness will flow abundantly, and all delights will be plentiful as the numberless motes of dust, and the whole world will be solely intent on the knowledge of the Lord. Therefore those of Israel will be great sages, who know what is hidden, and they will attain what knowledge of their Creator it is in man's power to attain, as it is written: "For the earth shall be full of the knowledge of the Lord, as the waters cover the sea."

THE DEBATE ON THE MESSIAH AT TORTOSA

Solomon ibn Verga

Spain—Italy, 15th–16th Century

FROM THE SHEBET YEHUDAH

This is a copy of the epistle that the great sage Abu Astruc sent to the holy congregation in Gerona, in the year 5173 [1413], to the effect that the great men in Israel were dis-

[1] *Ibid.*, 97 b.

tressed, and in trouble with the pope, because of a demand
of Joshua ha-Lorki's, whom the Christians, after he had
been converted to Christianity, called Maestro Geronimo
de Santa Fé—which, taking the initial letters, spells
megadef, that is, "blasphemer." For he had requested the
pope [1] to summon the wise men of Israel before him, so
that he, Maestro Geronimo, could then prove to them that
the Messiah had already come, and that Jesus was he; and
this he intended to prove from the Talmud. Now these
are the exact words of the epistle:

You, who are esteemed among the sons of Israel, you,
the nobles in Judah, who in your "houses and walls have
a monument and a name," where stood the stools for the
Torah and the testimony, where the stools for the Talmud
have stood from earliest times—may you always keep alive
the courage in your hearts. What you have known previously, know it now as well—that our helper "doth neither
slumber nor sleep," but saves us from those who scheme
evil toward us. A shoot that came forth from among us
thought to destroy us and to crush our religion down
to the very earth. For he, Joshua ha-Lorki, invented
thoughts to lead us astray, and to demonstrate that he was
in truth a Christian and was keeping the new faith. And
so he asked the pope to bid the chief among the wise men
of Jewry to come before him, for it was his purpose to
prove to us from our own Talmud that the Messiah had
already come. And he told the pope that after he had
proved this it would be legitimate to force the Jews to
accept the religion of Jesus, since he, Joshua, was going
to make all this true and apparent in the presence of His
Holiness. I, however, now come unto you to inform you
of all that has come to pass, and may you keep in mind
the details, so that you can reply to any heretic. Know
then that we have indeed escaped a danger that cannot be
gauged, for we were facing numerous bishops and grandees,
and many were eager to find us guilty.

The delegates had a meeting to decide who was to be
first to speak before the pope, and who was to begin with

[1] Benedict XIII, successor to Clement VII, the antipope, residing at
Avignon.

what, in their language, is called *arenga*. They all decided
that Don Vidal Benveniste was to begin, because he is
versed in all manner of knowledge, and can use the Latin
language. They also decided not to behave like the learned
Jews in the academies, where each interrupts the other's
word and scoffs at him if he does not agree, lest the pope
hold them in contempt, and also that they would address
Joshua ha-Lorki and the bishops with calm and courtesy.
None was to grow violent, not even if he were derided,
and each was to strengthen the courage of the other, so
that his heart might not sink.

Then we who were the delegates went to the pope with
the help of God, "who delivereth the poor from him that is
too strong for him," and the pope received us with an agreeable countenance, and wished to hear the names of the
places we came from, and asked each as to his name and
commanded all to be written down. At this we were greatly
alarmed and tried to discover the reason for it from the
scribe. He, however, told us that it boded no ill, for popes
and kings were wont to have everything that happened
during their lives written down in books, with due
accuracy.

Then the pope said to us: "You, who are esteemed
among the people of the Jews, a people that was chosen
by a Chooser who has existed from time immemorial, and
that, if it was rejected, was rejected because of its own
failings—have no fear of this debate, for no wrong and no
insult shall be done to you in my presence. Calm your
thoughts and speak with a firm heart; have no fear and do
not despair.

"Maestro Geronimo has said he wishes to prove that the
Messiah has already come, and to prove it from your own
Talmud. In our presence will it be shown whether truth
abides with his word, or whether he has dreamed a dream.
But you must not be afraid of him, because in a debate
there is one law for both sides. Go then, rest in your lodgings, and come to me again early tomorrow morning."

And forthwith he gave orders that we be given suitable
lodgings, and of the food he himself ate, or of that which
we are allowed to eat by the precepts of our law. And some

of us rejoiced at the pope's words, and others were sad thereat—as is usual with Jews.

On the second day we came before the pope and found the entire great hall, where the debate was to take place, tapestried in many colors, and seventy chairs set up for the bishops, who are called *cardinales, obispos,* and *arzobispos,* and all of these wore raiment embellished with gold. All the great men of Rome were there, and what with the burghers and the grandees, there were almost a thousand persons, and it was thus every day of the debate. And then our "hearts melted and became as water." Notwithstanding we said: "Blessed be he who has accorded of his glory to flesh and blood." [1]

Then the pope began to speak, saying: "You, who are the wise men among the Jews, know that I have not come here, nor did I send for you, to decide which of the two religions is the true, since I am well aware that my religion and my faith are the true, and that your Torah, while it once was true, has ceased to be so. You have been summoned only because Geronimo said he wanted to prove that the Messiah has already come, from the Talmud of your masters, who knew better than you. Therefore, speak only of this matter in my presence."

Then the pope turned his countenance upon Maestro Geronimo and said: "Do you begin the debate, and let them reply to you."

And Maestro Geronimo began: " 'Come now, and let us reason together, saith the Lord. . . . But if ye refuse and rebel, ye shall be devoured with the sword.' "

Then Don Vidal Benveniste began the *arenga* in the Latin tongue, and the pope took pleasure in his wisdom and his language. And in the course of his speech Don Vidal complained of Geronimo, saying that it was not right for one who wishes to debate, to begin by using hostile words, for he had said: " 'But if ye refuse and rebel, ye shall be devoured with the sword.' " He had proved nothing for the time being, and yet was setting himself up as a judge and avenger.

---

1 Benediction on seeing a king: Berakot 58 a.

At that the pope interposed: "You are right, but you must not be astonished at this evil way of his, for he was one of you."

The third day was the beginning of the debate proper, and Maestro Geronimo began, saying: "In your Talmud, it is said: 'Six thousand years is the span of the world—chaos,[1] two thousand years, Torah, two thousand years, and two thousand years, days of the Messiah.' [2] From this it is evident that the Messiah has come within the last two thousand years, and who could he be but our Savior?".

Ha-Lorki took a long time in talking on this subject, and preached to his heart's content, until the pope said to him: "Geronimo, it has been known to me for a long time that you are a great preacher; yet not because of this have we come together, but to hear you prove what you have promised. Therefore, have a care that you lose not yourself in preaching."

Then he turned his countenance upon the delegates and said: "Reply to the passage he cited."

And Don Vidal Benveniste spoke: "Sir, let us first consider the characteristics of the Messiah, and then it will become evident whether he has already come, and if what is written about the Messiah holds for him who has come, we too shall avow him."

And the pope said: "That is no answer to the question put to you, for what has been said did not concern the characteristics of the Messiah, but only the sentence saying that the Messiah has already come. You are following the manner of contentious Jews, who when one asks them about one thing, slip over to the next."

Thereupon Don Vidal answered him: "Sir, our beginning was in the manner of wise men, for it is proper to speak first of the nature of the matter in hand, and then

1 A period without a knowledge of the law. The end of this period is marked by the activity of Abraham, the first worshiper of God.

2 The Talmud (Sanhedrin 97 a) designates this saying as coming from the school of the prophet Elijah (Tanna debe Eliyahu). Geronimo considers this saying more credible than other Talmudic sayings, especially the explanatory addition, "But because of our iniquities, which were many, as much time has passed as has passed," which he regards as an invention of the "Talmudists."

of the particular circumstances; scientists also follow this rule. But if this way does not please you, our lord, we shall not take it. And so I shall now speak of the passage itself, and say that wise Geronimo extracted from it what he pleased, and what supports his point, but disregarded what contradicts it. For toward the end of the passage, we read: 'But because of our iniquities, which were many, as much time has passed as has passed,' and this clearly proves that he has not come."

Then Geronimo replied: "According to this, you have not understood the words, or you pretend not to have understood them. For 'And two thousand years, days of the Messiah' is the pronouncement of the prophet Elijah, who said it to his disciples—and these passed it on in his name —as a passage in the *Tanna debe Eliyahu* proves, and the Talmudists know this; now those disciples or men of the Talmud who included this passage in their books, are the ones who added, 'But because of our iniquities, which were many,' and they added it to substantiate their belief that Jesus was not the Messiah. But the prophet Elijah, being a prophet and knowing what was true, said only, 'And two thousand years, days of the Messiah,' in accordance with what he was aware of because of his gift of prophecy."

And Rabbi Zerahiah ha-Levi replied, saying: "It is probably more correct to assume that a passage originated with one man, rather than with two. When such is the case, the Talmud usually says: 'Rab Ashi, however, says,' or this one or that one says, 'But because of our iniquities, which were many.' That is why at the outset we said before our lord that we wanted to see if the characteristics of the Messiah apply or do not apply to him who has come, and for this reason: if the characteristics do apply to this person, then we will accept the passage according to Geronimo's interpretation; if the characteristics of the Messiah do not apply to him, then our interpretation is the true one."

And Geronimo replied: "But Elijah came long before the Jews went into exile, therefore we must necessarily say that the passage, 'Because of our iniquities, which were many,' was spoken by another, by one who was in exile.

And so it originated with the Talmudists, and, moreover, corresponds with their views, as I have already said."

Then Rabbi Joseph Albo [1] argued: "The Talmudists, through whom you are trying to disprove us, took that passage into the Talmud. But they would not have taken into it anything that was contrary to their views. Therefore, they believed that there were two possible periods of time for the Messiah—the time God has promised, or the time when Israel will be prepared and will turn to God. That is why the passage sets no time limit to the days of the Messiah, but speaks of 'two thousand years, days of the Messiah'—in other words, days prepared for the coming of the Messiah. If the Jews are worthy of him, he will come at the beginning; if they are not worthy at the beginning, but grow worthy within the period of time, the Messiah will come then. If they do not grow worthy within the period, but at the very end, then the Messiah will come at the end. But the two thousand years will not pass without his coming."

And the pope said: "Why do you not say that if the Christians are worthy of it he will come at once, but if not, that he will tarry until the end of the two thousand years?"

The delegates replied: "We believe that the redeemer will come only for the sake of those who are in exile. For he who lives in peace, does he require a redeemer? The Messiah is needed by a people that lives in exile and servitude."

Then Rabbi Matatiah said to Geronimo: "My wise sir, you prove from the Talmud that the Messiah has already come. Why, instead of this, do you not prove the contrary from that selfsame Talmud: For it says: 'Let the spirit of those breathe its last, who seek to calculate the end.' " [2]

But here the pope interposed, saying: "I have heard this before and should like to know what it is interpreted to mean."

And Rabbi Matatiah replied: "We have no interpretation of it, we follow the plain meaning in the words them-

1 Rabbi Joseph Albo represented the Jewish congregation of Daroca.

selves: A curse be upon him who makes calculations and declares precisely when the Messiah will come. This is very harmful to the people. For when the appointed time arrives, and he does not come, they fall into despair, and slack grow the hearts of those who hoped for weal and who were bound by the fetters and bonds of hope. And still another transgression is involved: God has hidden this thing from all peoples and from all prophets—yet this man is counting upon revealing it."

At this the pope was greatly angered, and said: "O people of fools, O foolish and despicable Talmudists! Does Daniel, for example, who calculated the term, deserve that it be said of him, 'Let his spirit breathe its last?' Truly, it appears that you are as sinful and rebellious as they."

Here Don Todros broke in, saying: "O sir, if the Talmudists are so foolish in your eyes, why do you refer to them to prove that the Messiah has already come? 'Nothing can be proved by fools.' " [1]

But at that the pope became still angrier. So Don Vidal took the floor and said conciliatingly: "It is not like His Holiness to be angered because of a matter that is being debated, especially since we were given freedom of speech. But we must have been guilty of some other thing, and so our words erred. And that is why we beg you, O lord, to give us your favor."

And with this we left on that day, and the next morning we went our way again. But when we arrived in our lodgings, a bitter quarrel broke out between us and Rabbi Matatiah and Rabbi Todros, because they had been so incautious and failed to rein their tongues.

Geronimo began with another passage,[2] [at the end of which] Rabbi Judan says: "It is written in the Scriptures: 'And Lebanon shall fall by a mighty one. And there shall come forth a shoot out of the stock of Jesse.' This verse clearly demonstrates that which you cannot deny, namely, that on the day the Temple was destroyed, the Messiah was born."

1 Shabbat 104 b.
2 Yerushalmi Berakot ii.

And the wise Abu Astruc replied: "This passage has been discussed by great men in this world, in the debate between Maestro Moses and Fra Paolo.[1] And Don Vidal said that at that time the maestro explained that it did not mean the Messiah had actually been born. But even if we did say that he had actually been born, this would not involve a contradiction, because it would be possible for him to be born on that day, but to live in the Garden of Eden. Rabbi Moses Maimonides also writes that the Messiah was not born on the day of the destruction of the Temple, but that the passage means that from that day on a man is born in every generation who would be worthy to be the Messiah, if Israel were worthy of it. And so he thinks that the purpose of these words was to goad hearts to turn to God, and to expound to them that the Messiah was not dependent upon a fixed time. And that is the way Don Hasdai explains it also." [2]

The pope replied angrily: "You have not come to my court to inform me of what your expounders say, but of what you yourselves say. Of what interest to me are the explanations of those who lived before you, all this vain and idle quibbling to the effect that he was indeed born, but is not as yet come! If this is dependent on the merits of the Jews, why was he born at all? This need not have come to pass, and he might have been born on the day on which they were prepared and worthy!"

And the delegates replied: "If they were worthy this very day, and if the Messiah were born this very day, could a child who is one day old lead them?"

The following morning the pope said: "You Jews, you say terrible things. What sensible man would say that the Messiah was, to be sure, born, but that he lived in the Garden of Eden for a long time, and that he has now been living for fourteen hundred years?"

Then Rabbi Astruc jumped up and said: "Sir, since you

[1] At Barcelona, 1263. Maestro Moses is Moses ben Nahman (Nahmanides). Cf. Index.
[2] Hasdai Crescas, 14th century, author of the book Or Adonai ("Light of the Lord"), a writer against Maimonides.

believe so many improbable things about your Messiah,
let us believe this one about our Messiah."

And the pope was so aroused by this that we feared his
bitter anger would break forth like a fire, and we said to
him: "Lord, what our comrade spoke was not fairly spoken
and not in agreement with all the rest of us, and he spoke
in jest, when he should not have done so, since the pope
is not one of us."

We went to our lodgings and we all screamed at Rabbi
Astruc, saying: "Our wrong be upon you! For you have
put the sword in the hands of our foes. We agreed not to
speak in the manner you have spoken. See, the pope was
favoring our cause, and he came to our assistance more
than to Geronimo's. But now that the pope is angered,
who will protect us, if not heaven in its mercy? But 'we
must not rely on miracles,' [1] where our own merit is so
dubious."

Thus on that day we left the hall derided and ashamed,
and the following morning we returned in great fear and
distress. But God granted that we were in favor, and we
found the pope with unclouded countenance.[2]

SABBATAI ZEVI

Glückel of Hameln

Germany, 17th–18th Century

FROM HER MEMOIRS

At this very time, they began to talk about Sabbatai Zevi,
but woe unto us that we have sinned, and that we did not
live to see the event. And how we listened, and how vividly
we pictured it! When I think of how they turned to God,
both the young and the old, I cannot describe it, but it
was known and bruited through the entire world.

1 Talmudic saying: Pesahim 64 b.
2 The disputation lasted one year and nine months (February 1413
to November 1414) and consumed sixty-nine sessions.

O Lord of the world, at the time we hoped that you,
merciful God, would have mercy upon your poor people
of Israel, and would deliver us, our hopes were quite like
those of a woman who sits upon the birthstool and suffers
great pains and pangs, and thinks that after all her pains
and pangs she will be gladdened with a child. Yet after all
her pains and pangs, nothing at all comes, save a wind.
And this, great God and King, is what has happened to
us also. We listened, and all your servants and your children, who are dear to you, strove devoutly with prayer
and turning and good works throughout the world. And
your beloved people of Israel sat upon the chair to give
birth and thought that after all this heavy turning and
prayer and good works—and when they had been sitting
upon the birthstool for two, for three years, after all of
this, nothing came but wind. It was not enough that we
were not found worthy to see the child for which we endured so much labor and had come so far that we felt sure
of it, and then, alas, stuck fast! Yet, my Lord God, your
people of Israel do not despair because of this, and they
hope, day for day, that you will be merciful, that you will
deliver them. "And though he delays, yet shall I hope each
day that he will come." [1] When your holy will prompts
you, you will surely remember your people of Israel.

It is impossible to describe what happiness prevailed
when letters were received. Most of the letters that arrived
were for the Sephardim, and they always took them to the
house of prayer in order to read them there. Germans also,
both young and old, went to join them in the house of
prayer. And the young men among the Portuguese always
donned their best raiment, and each wore a broad green
silk ribbon—that was Sabbatai Zevi's livery. And so they
all went to their house of prayer with timbrels and with
dances, to read the letters with joy.

Some, alas, sold all their worldly goods—their house and
all that belonged to it—and hoped every day that they
would be delivered. My father-in-law, peace be with him,
lived in Hameln; and he gave up his home there and left
behind his house and court and furnishings, and many

[1] One of the Thirteen Principles of Faith formulated by Maimonides.

good things, and moved to the city of Hildesheim, to reside there. And he sent to us, here in Hamburg, two large barrels with all kinds of linens. And inside there was every sort of food, such as peas, beans, dried meat, and many other things to eat, plum preserves, for instance, and all manner of foods that keep. For the good man, peace be with him, thought that it was quite simple to go from Hamburg straight to the Holy Land. These barrels remained in my house for over a year. Finally they grew afraid that the meat and the other things might spoil, so they wrote us to open the barrels and take out whatever there was to eat, lest the linen rot. And so it stood for about three years, and he always thought he would use it for his journey, but such was not the will of the Most High.

We know very well that it was promised to us by the Most High, and if we were completely devout, from the very depths of our hearts, and not so wicked, I am certain that the Omnipresent would have mercy upon us. If we only kept the commandment to love our neighbors as ourselves! But merciful God, how ill we keep it! The envy and senseless hatred that are betwixt us! These can make for nothing good. And yet, dear God, what you have promised us, that you will give us, in kingliness and grace. Though it delays so long in coming, because of our sins, we shall surely have it when the appointed time is come. And on this we will set our hopes, and pray to you, almighty God, that you may at last gladden us with perfect redemption.

THE KINGDOM OF GOD

Rab

Babylonia, 2d–3d Century

FROM THE PRAYER BOOK

It is for us
to praise the Lord of all,
to acclaim the greatness of him
who shaped the world in the beginning,
for that he has not made us
like the peoples of other lands,
nor set us level with
the clans of earth,
nor fixed our share
to equal theirs,
our lot
to match their crowd and clamor.
For we bend the knee,
prostrate ourselves,
give thanks
before the King
over kings of kings,
the Holy, blessed be he,
who unfurls the sky,
and founds the earth;
his seat of glory
is in the heavens above,
the house of his might
is on majestic heights.
He is our God,
there is none else.
Truly he is our King,
and there is none beside.
As it is written in his Torah:
"Know this day, and lay it to thy heart,
that the Lord, He is God
in heaven above
and upon the earth beneath;
there is none else."

And so we wait for you,
Lord our God,
we wait soon to see the splendor of your might
when you will raze the idols from the earth,
so that false gods be stricken and stricken out,
when the world will be perfected under the kingdom of the
    Almighty,
so that all flesh shall call your name,
when you will turn to you all the wicked on this earth.
All dwellers in the world shall see and know
that every knee is bowed to you,
and every tongue avows you.
Before you, Lord our God, they shall kneel and cast them-
    selves on their faces,
to give honor
to the glory of your name.
They all will take upon themselves
the yoke of your kingdom,
and you will be King over them
soon, for ever and ever.
For the kingdom,
it is yours,
and in all time and all eternity
you will govern in glory.
As it is written in your Torah:
"The Lord shall reign
for ever and ever."
And it is said:
"And the Lord shall be King over all the earth;
in that day
shall the Lord be One,
and His name one."

SOURCES

I

p. 17. How we shall serve: as quoted in M. Buber, Des Baal-Schem-Tow Unterweisung im Umgang mit Gott, Bücherei des Schocken Verlages no. 21, p. 39.

p. 17. God, world, man: as quoted in M. Buber, Die Chassidischen Bücher, Berlin: Schocken, 1928, pp. 31-36 (selected).

p. 19. Between man and God: The blessing, Berakot 28 b; Big and small, Genesis Rabbah IV, 3; In common use, Numbers Rabbah XV, 6; The service of God, Pesikta Rabbati XXV, Friedmann 127 a; The righteous, Numbers Rabbah VIII, 2; The direction, Mishnah Rosh ha-Shanah III, 8; Wages, Sayings of the Fathers I, 3; His, Sayings of the Fathers III, 7; The steps of man, Mekilta on Exodus 17, 6, Friedmann 52 b; Every day, Seder Eliyahu Rabbah II, Friedmann p. 8; The whole, Genesis Rabbah X, 8; Man and thing, Sayings of the Fathers IV, 3.

p. 23. The face of man: Zohar, Genesis fol. 71 a.

p. 25. Design in the universe: Maimonides, Moreh Nebukim III, 12.

p. 30. Door within door: Zohar, Genesis fol. 103 a-b (transl. by Sperling and Simon, London: Soncino, 1931, I, 331-32).

p. 32. Peace: Perek ha-Shalom, in Talmud editions. Cf. Numbers Rabbah XI, 16-20.

II

p. 34. On hiding from the presence of God: Philo, Legum sacrarum allegoriarum libri III, 1-6, 28-31 (notes adapted from Isaak Heinemann, Die Werke Philos von Alexandria, Breslau, 1919, III).

p. 37. The good name: Berakot 17 a.

p. 39. The devout: Judah ha-Levi, Kuzari III, 2-5.

p. 41. The world of those who love God: Bahya ibn Pakuda, Hobot ha-Lebabot X, 7.

p. 47. For the sake of truth: Maimonides, Commentary on the Mishnah, Sanhedrin X.

p. 51. The root of the love of God: Eleazar ben Judah, Sefer ha-Rokeah, Intro. fol. 3.

p. 52. You stand before the Lord: Nahmanides, Commentary on the Pentateuch, Lisbon, 1489, App.; also in Yehiel Milli, Tappuhe Zahab, Mantua, 1623.

p. 55. Hanina ben Dosa: Food, Bread, Poverty, Faith, The rain, Taanit 24 b-25 b; Sin, Berakot 33 a; The righteous and his beast, Abot de R. Nathan VIII, Schechter p. 38; Effectual prayer, Berakot 34 b; Dignity of creatures, Tanhuma on Gen. 44:18; The end, Sotah 49 b.

p. 58. Susia of Hanipol: as quoted in M. Buber, Die Chassidischen Bücher, Berlin: Schocken, 1928, pp. 430-42 (selected).

p. 63. The death through the kiss of God: Maimonides, Moreh Nebukim III, 51, last part.

III

p. 65. Freedom of will: Maimonides, Mishneh Torah, Hilkot Teshubah V.

p. 68. Of the ways of life: After the destruction of the Temple, Abot de R. Nathan IV, Schechter p. 21; Blood, Pesahim 25 b; The causes of suffering, Berakot 5 a; Disaster, Berakot 60 a; Suppositions, Seder Eliyahu Rabbah VI, Friedmann p. 31; Ascent, Abodah Zarah 20 b; The monuments of the righteous, Yerushalmi, Shekalim 9 b; The crown of creation, Sanhedrin 38 a; Arrogance, Sotah 5 a; Worthy of life, Berakot 28 b.

p. 71. The sacrifice of Abraham: Abraham ben David ha-Levi, ha-Emunah ha-Ramah, ed. S. Weil, Frankfurt a.M., 1852, pp. 103-4 (transl. by S. Kurland).

p. 72. Man's intent: Joseph Karo, Shulhan Aruk, Orah Hayyim no. 231.

p. 74. The proof: Hayyim ibn Musa, in Weiss and Friedmann, Bet Talmud II (1882), 117.

p. 75. The foundation of devoutness: Moses Hayyim

Luzatto, Mesillat Yesharim, Amsterdam, 1740, I.

p. 79. Open thou my lips: Zechariah Mendel of Jaroslav, Darke Zedek 40-50.

p.81. The order of the Essenes, Flavius Josephus, Bellum Judaicum II, 8.2-11.

p. 86. The end-all of knowledge: as quoted in M. Buber, Des Baal-Schem-Tow Unterweisung (cf. above), pp. 16-19.

IV

p. 88. The herdsman who could not pray: Sefer Hasidim, ed. by Jehuda Wistinetzki, Berlin, 1891, 4-6.

p. 89. Prayers of the Masters: Berakot 16 b-17 a.

p. 91. The soul you have given me: Berakot 60 b; Prayer Book.

p. 92. Grace after meals: Prayer Book.

p. 92. From darkness to light: Prayer Book (Singer).

p. 93. The end of the Sabbath: Prayer Book.

p. 94. Invocation: Eser Orot, Petrokov, 1907, XXIV, i.

p. 95. In judgment: Prayer Book (Singer).

V

p. 96. Sinning and turning: Sinners and sin, Berakot 10 a; You yourself, Tanhuma on Gen. 3:22; Ironwork, Abot de R. Nathan XVI, Schechter p. 64; Fire and flesh, Kiddushin 81 a; Today, Shabbat 153 a; The place of those who turn to God, Berakot 34 b.

p. 98. The building of the Temple and the wedding feast: Leviticus Rabbah XII, 4; Numbers Rabbah X, 8.

p. 99. Elisha ben Abuyah, the apostate: Hagigah 15 a-b; Yerushalmi, Hagigah II, 1.

p. 103. The doctrine of turning: Maimonides, Mishneh Torah, Hilkot Teshubah II.

p. *106.* Worse than sin: mentioned by Isaac Judah Yehiel in Hekal ha-Berakah, as quoted in S. J. Agnon, Yamim Noraim, Berlin: Schocken, 1938, p. 206.

p. 107. On pride and on the nature of evil: Israel Baal Shem, as quoted in M. Buber, Des Baal-Schem-Tow Unterweisung (cf. above), pp. 85, 93, 96.

p. 108. Messengers: Nahman of Bratzlav, as quoted in M. Buber, Die Chassidischen Bücher (cf. above), pp. 34, 35.

p. 108. Tales of the turning: *ibid.* pp. 629-37 (selected).

p. 110. Sermon on the Day of Atonement: *ibid.* p. 637 f.

p. 111. The voice from heaven: as quoted by M. Buber in Almanach des Schocken Verlages 5695, p. 50.

VI

p. 113. Concerning the learning of children: Zevi Hirsh Kaidanower, Kab ha-Yashar, Frankfurt a.M., 1705, chap. LXXII.

p. 116. The journey: Jacob ben Wolf Kranz, Ohel Yaakob, Jozefow, 1830, App.

p. 117. The honor due to parents: On a par, The three, Honor and fear, How far, The Steps, Kiddushin 30 b-31 b; Honor due to parents and to God, Yerushalmi Peah I,1; Service, *ibid.;* The mother, Deuteronomy Rabbah I,14; Precedence, Horayot 13 a.

p. 121. On the precept of honoring one's parents: Joseph Karo, Shulhan Aruk, Yoreh Deah no. 240.

p. 124. The mission of woman: Jonah ben Abraham Gerondi, Iggeret ha-Teshubah, Kraków, 1586, Sixth Day.

VII

p. 126. The teaching and the teachers: The keepers, Pesikta de R. Kahana 120 b; The decisions, Erubin 13 b; The tool, Abot de R. Nathan XXII, Schechter p. 74; Heredity, Nedarim 81 a; Scholars and kings, Horayot 13 a; What animals teach, Erubin 100 b; The death of Rabbi Simeon ben Lakish, Baba Metzia 84 a; Feeding the hungry, Baba Batra 8 a; The task, Sayings of the Fathers II,16.

p. 129. The commandments are one: Makkot 23 b-24 a.

p. 131. Law and justice: Baba Metzia 83 a.

p. 131. Not in heaven: *ibid.* 59 a.

p. 132. The allegory of the lover: Zohar, Exodus fol. 99 a-b (transl. by Sperling and Simon, London: Soncino, 1931, III, 301-2.

p. 134. On books and on writing: text and transl. in Israel Abrahams, Hebrew Ethical Wills (Philadelphia: Jewish Publication Soc., 1926), chap. III (selected).

p. 137. A collector of books: Joseph Solomon del Medigo, Melo Hofnayim, ed. by Abraham Geiger, Berlin, 1840.

p. *139.* Good and bad books: Joseph Solomon del Medigo, Noblot Hokmah, Basel, 1629, fol. 7 b-8 a.

p. 141. In farewell: Berakot 17 a.

VIII

p. 142. From man to man: Nahman of Bratzlav, as quoted in M. Buber, Die Chassidischen Bücher (cf. above), p. 35.

p. 142. Mercy upon living creatures: The sufferings of Rabbi Judah the Prince, Baba Metzia 85 a; The shepherds, Exodus Rabbah II, 2; The creation of the world, Genesis Rabbah XII, 15, Rashi on Gen. 1:1; The imitation of God, Sotah 14 a.

p. 145. The love of one's neighbor and the love of God: Samuel Laniado, Kli Hemdah, Venice, 1596, on Lev. 19:18.

p. 147. The ugly implement: Derek Erez Rabbah in Talmud editions.

p. 148. The true physician: Harry Friedenwald, The Jews and Medicine, Baltimore: Johns Hopkins Press, 1944, I, 22-23.

p. 151. The diseased wife: Teshubot Rashi, ed. by I. Elfenbein, New York, 1943, pp. 232-33 (transl. by S. Kurland).

p. 152. The servant: Maimonides, Mishneh Torah, Hilkot Abadim IX (transl. by S. Kurland).

p. 153. A story of the rich man and the beggar: Maasiyot, ed. by A. Jellinek, Bet ha-Midrash, Vienna, 1872, V, 138-39.

p. 155. Concerning hatred: Jacob ben Wolf Kranz, Sefer ha-Middot, Johannesburg, 1859, chap. VII, p. 4.

p. 159. On gossip and hatred: Iggeret ha-Teshubah, Kraków, 1586, Second Day.

p. *160.* The poor man: Admittance of the king, Baba Batra 10 a; The poorer man, Nedarim 50 a; I and he, Leviticus Rabbah XXXIV, 16; God's people, Exodus Rabbah XXXI, 5.

IX

p. 162. Israel: The burning bush, Exodus Rabbah II, 9; Dust and star, Megillah 16 a; God chooses the oppressed, Leviticus Rabbah XXVII, 5; Like oil, Canticles Rabbah I, 21; The need of Israel and the need of peoples, Deuteronomy Rabbah II, 14, Exodus Rabbah XXIII, 8; The open gate, Exodus Rabbah XIX, 4; Doing, Seder Eliyahu Rabbah IX, Friedmann p. 48.

p. 166. The heart of the nations: Judah ha-Levi, Kuzari II, 36-44.

p. 168. The survival of Israel: Maimonides, Iggeret Teman, in Kobetz Teshubot ha-Rambam, Leipzig, 1859 II, 1-3 (transl. by N. Glatzer, in Maimonides Said, New York: Jewish Book Club, 1941, pp. 63-65).

p. 170. The ascending flame: Zohar, Genesis fol. 50 b-51 a (transl. by Sperling and Simon, London: Soncino, 1931, I, 162-63.

p. 172. The proselyte: Maimonides, Teshubot ha-Rambam, ed. by A. Freimann, Jerusalem, 1934, no. 42 (transl. by N. Glatzer, in Maimonides Said (cf. above), pp. 57-59).

p. 173. The parable of the seed: Judah ha-Levi, Kuzari IV, 20-23.

X

p. 176. To die as free men: Flavius Josephus, Bellum Judaicum VII, 8.6-7; 9.1.

p. 179. The ten martyrs: Asarah Haruge Malkut, in Bet

ha-Midrash, ed. by A. Jellinek, vol. VI; Midrash Ele Ezkera, *ibid.*, vol. II, Sanhedrin 14 a, Abodah Zarah 17 b-18 b, Semahot VIII, other sources; compilation of documents by M. J. bin Gurion adopted in part (Die zehn Märtyrer, Bücherei des Schocken Verlages no. 32, Berlin, 1935).

p. 187. Persecutions at the time of the first crusade: Solomon bar Simeon, in Hebräische Berichte über die Judenverfolgungen während der Kreuzzüge, ed. by A. Neubauer and M. Stern, Berlin, 1892, pp. 1-14 (selected).

p. 190. Hallowing the name of God: Maimonides, Mishneh Torah, Hilkot Yesode ha-Torah V, 1-4.

p. 192. Emigration: Maimonides, Maamar Kiddush ha-Shem, in Kobetz Teshubot ha-Rambam, Leipzig, 1859, II, 15.

p. 193. Expulsion from Spain: Isaac ben Judah Abrabanel, Perush Neviim Rishonim, Naples, 1543, Books of Kings, Intro.

p. 198. They shall wander from sea to sea: Judah ben Jacob Hayyat, Minhat Yehudah, commentary on Maareket ha-Elohut of Perez ben Isaac ha-Kohen, Mantua, 1558, Pref. fol. 4-5 (transl. by S. Kurland).

p. 201. The death of the martyrs: fragment from Megillat Amraphel, ed. by Gershom Scholem in Kiryath Sepher VII (Jerusalem, 1930-31), 153-55 (a German translation by editor in Aus Unbekannten Schriften, Berlin, 1928, pp. 89-94).

p. 204. A Jew I shall remain: Solomon ibn Verga, Shebet Yehudah, ed. by M. Wiener, Hanover, 1856, chap. LII (transl. by S. Kurland).

p. 205. The supreme sacrifice: Alexander Süsskind, Zavaa, Grodno, 1794 (transl. in Israel Abrahams, Hebrew Ethical Wills, Philadelphia: Jewish Publication Soc., 1926, p. 330).

XI

p. 206. The holy land of Israel: Nahman of Bratzlav, Likkute Mohoran, Ostrów, 1808; selections as quoted by M. Buber in Almanach des Schocken Verlags 5697, pp. 62-64.

p. 207. The sacred place: Judah ha-Levi, Kuzari V, 22-28 (transl. from Arabic by H. Hirschfeld, New York, 1927, used in part).

p. 209. Within the gates of desolate Jerusalem: Nahmanides, Commentary on the Pentateuch, Lisbon, 1489, App. (transl. by S. Kurland).

p. 210. The land is blessed: *Ibid.*

p. 211. The agreement: Asher ben Yehiel, Teshubot, Constantinople, 1522, VIII, 13.

p. 213. The strength of wanting: Shibhe ha-Ari, Shklov, 1795; quoted in Abraham Kahana, Sifrut ha-Historia ha-Yisraelit, Warsaw, 1923, II, 212.

p. 214. In Jerusalem: Obadiah of Bertinoro, Letters, ed. by S. Sachs in Jahrbuch für die Geschichte der Juden, III (Leipzig, 1863), 195-224.

p. 216. Zion forgotten: Jacob Emden, Bet Yaakob, Lemberg, 1901, Intro.

p. 217. How to enter the Holy Land: Abraham Kalisker, Pri ha-Aretz, Kopys, 1814, App.

XII

p. 219. Before the gates of Rome: Sanhedrin 98 a.

p. 220. The suffering servant: Zohar, Exodus fol. 212 a.

p. 220. Messiah, the Anointed King: Maïmonides, Mishneh Torah, Hilkot Melakim XI-XII.

p. 223. The debate on the Messiah at Tortosa: Solomon ibn Verga, Shebet Yehudah, ed. by M. Wiener, Hanover, 1856, chap. XL.

p. 232. Sabbatai Zevi: Glückel of Hameln, Memoirs, ed. by David Kaufmann, Frankfurt a.M., 1896, pp. 80-83.

p. 234. The kingdom of God: *Alenu* hymn (presumably composed by Rab), Prayer Book.

AUTHORS AND WORKS

ABRAHAM KALISKER: 18th cent. Disciple of Rabbi Elijahu of Wilno, outstanding talmudist, later of Dob Baer of Meseritz, hasidic rabbi; rabbi of Kaliska (Poland); settled in Palestine in 1777, becoming leader of hasidic group there.

ABRAHAM BEN DAVID HA-LEVI: b. ca. 1110, Toledo, d. ca. 1170. Historian, philosopher, astronomer, martyr; harmonized Aristotelian system with Judaism. Author of *Ha-Emunah ha-Ramah* ("Exalted Faith") in Arabic, 1161; forerunner of Maimonides.

ABRAHAM BEN ELIEZER HA-LEVI: b. ca. 1460, Spain, d. ca. 1530. Among exiles from Spain, 1492; eminent mystic. Author of *Megillat Amraphel.*

ALEXANDER (BEN MOSES) SÜSSKIND: d. 1794, Grodno, Lithuania. Rabbinical scholar. Author of liturgical work, *Yesod ve-Shoresh ha-Abodah* ("Basis and Root of Service").

ASAPH JUDAEUS: 7th cent., Mesopotamia. Author of the oldest medical writings in Hebrew.

BAHYA (BEN JOSEPH) IBN PAKUDA: Saragossa, 11th and possibly 12th cent. Author of *Hobot ha-Lebabot* ("Duties of the Heart") in Arabic, 1040, first extensive Jewish system of ethics, marked by trend to mysticism and asceticism.

DEREK EREZ RABBAH: *cf.* Talmud.

ELEAZAR BEN JUDAH: b. ca. 1176, Speyer, Germany, d. 1238, Worms, Germany. Disciple of Judah he-Hasid; talmudist, liturgical poet, mystic. Author of *Rokeah*, ethical work documenting deep love for God and mankind.

ELISHA BEN ABUYAH: b. Jerusalem before 70 C. E. Talmudic sage (tanna); teacher of Rabbi Meir; under influence of foreign, probably gnostic teachings, deserted pharisaic Judaism, hence called *Aher* ("the other").

FLAVIUS JOSEPHUS: b. 37 C. E., Jerusalem, d. ca. 120, Rome. Descendant of Hasmoneans; commander in Galilee at beginning of Jewish war against Romans (67 C. E.), later surrendering. Wrote, in Rome, *History of the Jewish War* (in Greek), completed before 79 C. E., and *Antiquities of the Jews* (in Greek) 93 C. E.

GLÜCKEL OF HAMELN: b. 1646 Hamburg, d. 1724, Metz. Beginning 1690, wrote her memoirs (in Judaeo-German), valuable representation of Jewish life in her time.

HANINA BEN DOSA: talmudic sage (tanna) and saint, Palestine, 1st cent. Disciple of Johanan ben Zakkai.

HAYYIM IBN MUSA: b. ca. 1390, Bejar, Spain, d. 1460. Apologist and physician. Author of *Magen wa-Romah*, 1456, apology for Judaism against accusations of church.

ISAAC BEN JUDAH ABRABANEL: b. 1437, Lisbon, d. 1508, Venice. Statesman, biblical commentator, philosophical writer; lived from 1483 in Toledo; 1492 (expulsion of Jews from Spain) fled to Naples, later to Venice. In his works, tries to harmonize mystical and rationalist systems.

ISAAC BEN JUDAH IBN GHAYYAT: b. 1038, Lucena, Spain, d. 1089, Cordova. Liturgical poet, rabbinical authority, philosopher. Author of work on ritual laws, *Shaare Simhah*.

ISAAC (BEN SOLOMON ASHKENAZI) LURIA: b. 1534, Jerusalem, d. 1572, Safed, Palestine. Leader of Safed kabbalistic movement; outstanding authority in later Jewish mysticism. His system was compiled by his great follower, Hayyim Vital Calabrese (1543-1620), in *Etz Hayyim* ("The Tree of Life").

ISAAC MEIR (BEN ISRAEL) OF GER ("GERER RABBI"): b. Gora Kalwaria, n. Warsaw, d. 1866. Hasidic rabbi of great influence, disciple of Rabbi Simha Bunam of Pshysha; talmudic scholar. Author of *Hiddushe Rim*.

ISAAC OF WORKI: d. 1848. Hasidic rabbi, disciple of Rabbi Simha Bunam of Pshysha.

ISRAEL (BEN ELIEZER) BAAL SHEM ("MASTER OF THE HOLY NAME"): b. 1700, Okop, Podolia, d. 1760, Miedzyboz, Podolia. Founder of Hasidism, religious movement in eastern Europe, 18th cent., aiming at revival of faith and personal piety as against overemphasis on intellect and ritual as in rabbinical orthodoxy. Chief disciple and propagator of his teachings was Dob Baer of Meseritz ("the Great Maggid").

JACOB BEN HANANEL: 13th and 14th cent., Cordova.

JACOB (BEN ZEVI) EMDEN: b. 1697, Altona, Germany, d. Altona 1776. Talmudic scholar; opponent and critic of Sabbatianic doctrine. Author of many rabbinical works, among them commentary on Prayer Book.

JACOB BEN WOLF KRANZ ("DUBNER MAGGID"): b. ca. 1740 Zietil, gov. Wilno, d. 1804, Zamosc. Preacher (maggid) of great renown. Principal works: *Ohel Yaakob,* commentary on Pentateuch; *Sefer ha-Middot,* ethical work.

JONAH BEN ABRAHAM GERONDI: b. Gerona, Spain, d. 1263, Toledo. Among great talmudic teachers of his time; opposed philosophy of Maimonides. Author of ethical treatise, *Iggeret ha-Teshubah.*

JOSEPH (BEN EPHRAIM) KARO: b. 1488, Spain or Portugal, d. 1575, Safed, Palestine. Author of *Shulhan Aruk,* which became representative code of rabbinical Judaism.

JOSEPH SOLOMON (BEN ELIJAH) DEL MEDIGO: b. 1591, Candia, Crete, d. 1655, Prague. Physician, philosopher, astronomer (pupil of Galileo). Author of many scientific books and essays, among them *Elim.*

JUDAH BEN JACOB HAYYAT: b. 15th cent. Spain. Kabbalist; among exiles from Spain, 1492; after long wanderings, settled in Mantua. Author of commentary on kabbalistic system *Maareket ha-Elohut* ("Order of God"), by Perez ben Isaac ha-Kohen.

JUDAH (BEN SAMUEL) HE-HASID: d. 1217, Regensburg. Mystic and poet; leader in medieval German Hasidism. Principal work, Sefer Hasidim ("Book of the Devout") comprises ethical, mystical, and ascetic teachings.

JUDAH (BEN SAMUEL) HA-LEVI: b. ca. 1085, Toledo, d. Palestine after 1141. Philosopher, poet, physician. Principal works: religious and secular Hebrew poetry; *Kuzari* (in Arabic), dialogue between heathen king of Chazars and Jewish master, on revealed religions and position of

Judaism; representative of theological thinking in Middle Ages; greatest post biblical Hebrew poet.

JUDAH (BEN SAUL) IBN TIBBON: b. ca. 1120, Granada, d. after 1190. Physician, Lunel, France. Famous as translator (Arabic to Hebrew) of philosophical and ethical works of Saadia, Bahya ibn Pakuda, Solomon ibn Gabirol, Judah ha-Levi, others.

LEVI ISAAC OF BERDITSHEV: b. 1740, Husakow, Galicia, d. 1809. Berditshev. Hasidic rabbi, disciple of Dob Baer of Meseritz ("the Great Maggid"); devoted his life to love of God and Israel.

LUZATTO, MOSES HAYYIM: b. 1707, Padua, d. 1747, Safed, Palestine. Mystic, poet. Author of *Mesillat Yesharim* ("Path of the Upright"), 1740, work on religious ethics.

MAASIYOT: popular collections of stories, legends, tales, originating in different times and countries. One group of *Massiyot* has been edited by A. Jellinek, in his *Bet ha-Midrash*, Vol. v.

MAIMONIDES (MOSES BEN MAIMON; RAMBAM): b. 1135, Cordova, d. 1204, Cairo. Talmudist, philosopher, physician; foremost Jewish thinker of Middle Ages. Principal works: *Commentary* on *Mishnah* (in Arabic); code of law, *Mishneh Torah* ("Double of the Torah"), first systematic exposition of Jewish religion; *Moreh Nebukim* ("Guide of the Perplexed"), representative theological work (in Arabic); responsa and epistles; treatises on medicine.

MIDRASH ("INVESTIGATION"; "EXPOSITION"): exegesis of Scriptures, especially of nonlegal portions (*Midrash Haggadah*), compiled in talmudic period and in following centuries. Midrashic collections (very often in form of commentary on Scriptures or on single books of Bible) include, e.g., *Midrash Rabbah, Midrash Tanhuma, Pesikta Rabbati, Pesikta de Rab Kahana, Tanna debe Eliyahu.*

NAHMAN (BEN SIMHA) OF BRATZLAV: b. 1771, Miedzyboz, Podolia, d. 1810, Uman, Ukraine. Greatgrandson of Israel Baal Shem; aimed at renaissance of original hasidism; founder of distinct branch of hasidism bearing his name.

His teachings were published by his disciple, Nathan, in *Likkute Mohoran.*

NAHMANIDES (MOSES BEN NAHMAN; RAMBAN): b. ca. 1195, Gerona, Spain, d. Acre, ca. 1270. Talmudist, Bible exegete, mystic, physician; opposed Maimonides' rationalist philosophy; participated in religious disputation at Barcelona, 1263. Author of commentaries on Bible and Talmud.

OBADIAH (BEN ABRAHAM) OF BERTINORO: lived second part 15th cent., Bertinoro, Italy; d. ca. 1500, Jerusalem. Famous commentator on Mishnah. Wrote travel descriptions that are of great interest in relation to history of Jews in Greece, Egypt, Palestine.

PEREK HA-SHALOM: *cf.* Talmud.

PHILO: ca. 25 B. C. E.-40 C. E., Alexandria, Egypt. Jewish neo-Platonic philosopher, whose teachings influenced development of early Christian doctrines. Principal works, allegorical commentaries on Pentateuch (in Greek).

RAB (ABBA AREKA): b. ca. 175 C. E., Kafri, Babylonia, d. 247 C. E. Talmudic sage (amora); disciple of Rabbi Judah the Prince (compiler of Mishnah); with Mar Samuel, founded Jewish learning in Babylonia; established talmudic academy in Sura, Babylonia, which existed about eight hundred years. Author of liturgical poems.

SAMUEL (BEN ABRAHAM) LANIADO: second part 16th cent., Aleppo, Syria. Author of midrashic commentaries on Bible.

SIMLAI: b. 3d cent., Nehardea, Babylonia; lived in Palestine. Talmudic sage (amora), distinguished haggadic thinker.

SOLOMON BEN ISAAC (RASHI): b. 1040, Troyes, France, d. Troyes, 1105. Lived in Worms, Germany. His commentaries on Bible and Talmud are of utmost importance for understanding of Jewish tradition; his method of interpretation gave rise talmudic school of Tosafists.

SOLOMON BEN SAMPSON: wrote at Mayence, Germany, 1140, account of persecutions of Jews in time of first crusade, using written sources and oral traditions.

SOLOMON IBN VERGA: b. Seville, Spain, 15th cent., d. Naples
(?). Physician and historical writer; among exiles from
Spain, 1492. Author of *Shebet Yehudah,* containing valuable accounts of persecutions of Jews and of Jewish-Chris-
tian theological debates in Middle Ages.

SUSIA OF HANIPOL: d. 1809. Hasidic rabbi, saint; disciple
of Dob Baer of Meseritz (the "Great Maggid").

TALMUD ("TEACHING"): consists of (1) Mishnah ("Repeti-
tion"), code compiled by Rabbi Judah the Prince (called
"Rabbi") ca. 200, (2) Gemara ("Completion"), discussion
of Mishnah in academies of Palestine (Talmud Yerushalmi
or Palestinian Talmud, compiled ca. end 4th cent.) and
Babylonia (Talmud Babli or Babylonian Talmud, compiled ca. end 5th cent.). Sages and masters quoted in Mishnah are called tannaim (singular, tanna); those quoted in
Gemara, amoraim (singular, amora). Sections dealing with
law are called halakah ("conduct"; "guidance"; "law"),
those devoted to other subjects, especially to biblical
exegesis, haggadah (or aggadah; "narrative"). Among
treatises dealing with ethics are Mishnah tractate *Abot*
("Sayings of the Fathers"), and *Derek Erez Rabbah, Derek
Erez Zuta* with *Perek ha-Shalom* (collections accompanying Babylonian Talmud). Language of Mishnah is Hebrew; of Gemara, Aramaic and in part Hebrew.

ZECHARIAH MENDEL OF JAROSLAV: 18th cent. hasidic rabbi.

ZEVI HIRSH KAIDANOVER: b. Wilno, d. 1712, Frankfurt a.M.
Rabbi. Author of book on ethics, *Kab ha-Yashar.*

ZOHAR (*Sefer ha-Zohar,* "BOOK OF SPLENDOR"): foremost
work of Jewish mysticism, composed in Aramaic, as commentary on Pentateuch; represents Jewish form of theos-
ophy. Tradition ascribes its origin to Rabbi Simeon ben
Yohai (Palestine, 2d cent.). Its author was Moses de Leon,
great Spanish kabbalist, 13th cent.

LIST OF BIBLICAL QUOTATIONS

Arranged in the sequence of their appearance

SUGGESTIONS FOR FURTHER READING

Abrahams, Israel, *Jewish Life in the Middle Ages*. New Edition, by Cecil Roth. London, 1932

Adler, Morris, *The World of the Talmud* (A Hillel Little Book). Washington, 1959

Agus, Jacob B., *The Evolution of Jewish Thought*. New York, 1959

Baron, Salo W., *A Social and Religious History of the Jews*, I-VIII, Philadelphia, 1952-1960

Finkelstein, Louis, ed., *The Jews*, I-II, 3rd ed., Philadelphia, 1960 (esp. the essays "The Historical Foundations of Post-biblical Judaism" (Elias J. Bickerman), "The Period of the Talmud" (Judah Goldin), "On Medieval Hebrew Poetry" (Shalom Spiegel), "The Mystical Element in Judaism" (Abraham J. Heschel), and "Judaism and World Philosophy" (Alexander Altmann)

Glatzer, Nahum N., ed., *Jerusalem and Rome: From the Writings of Josephus*, New York, 1960

Hertz, Joseph Herman, *Commentary on the Prayer Book*

Kobler, Franz, ed., *A Treasury of Jewish Letters*, 2 vols., Philadelphia, 1954

Marcus, Jacob R., *The Jew in the Medieval World*, Cincinnati, 1938; paperback edition, Philadelphia, 1960

Montefiore, C. G., and Loewe, H., ed., *A Rabbinic Anthology*, London, 1938, and Philadelphia, 1960

Moore, George F., *Judaism in the First Centuries of the Christian Era*, 3 vols., Cambridge, Mass., 1927-1930

Newman, Louis I., *The Hasidic Anthology*, New York, 1944

Noveck, Simon, ed., *Great Jewish Personalities in Ancient and Medieval Times*, New York, 1959

Roth, Leon, *Judaism, A Portrait*, New York, 1961

Scholem, Gershom G., *Major Trends in Jewish Mysticism*, New York, 1954; paperback edition, New York, 1961

Schwarz, Leo W., ed., *Great Ages and Ideas of the Jewish People*, New York, 1956

Waxman, Meir, *A History of Jewish Literature*, I-II, 2nd ed., New York, 1960

INDEX OF TOPICS AND TYPES
OF LITERATURE

I. TOPICS

II. TYPES OF LITERATURE

808 Paperback

Glatzer, Nahum N Copy 1

A Jewish Reader

DATE DUE		

808 Paperback

Glatzer, Nahum N.

AUTHOR

A Jewish Reader Copy 1

TITLE

DATE DUE	BORROWER'S NAME	ROOM NUMBER
5/11/81	Eric Cantor	8
	confirm	

Temple Beth-El Library
Great Neck, N. Y.